EXPOSING INTERNET FRAUDSTERS

AN INSIDE REVELATION

BY

ISRAEL NNACHI UKA

DISCLAIMER

Table of Contents

DEDICATION

I dedicate this book to LISA. She made it possible with her love and support. She is truly an ANGEL!!

PREFACE

In this book we shall beam our search light on internet fraud. Criminal Minds have mastered the art of ripping off people's hard earned money. The joy of meeting and making new friends often turn sour in the mouth of millions of unsuspecting victims of internet scam. It's happening every day and will likely continue unless something is done to curb this ravaging menace. There are so many ways and means these Criminal Minds deploy to actualize their dubious aim. The internet is meant to create a platform to socialize and interact with the global community. **_When people become too trusty, they become victims of so many who are not trustworthy._** These are cold blooded fraudsters who are willing to con people of their last penny. So mean they don't care about the consequences of their actions on the lives of their victims.

Their code is just to get rich at others expense and peril. Many victims who didn't take their ugly ordeal well have most times ended up taking their own lives. So many others are too shocked to even talk about their sad tales. Some others will prefer to keep to themselves to avoid being perceived as fools by those who will hear their story. This has been a great impediment to the fight against this crime. How will you fight when people who are affected don't speak up? It's like they prefer dying in silence. But this book is borne out of the good-will to help those who are affected and to prevent others from being affected. This is not a fictional novel or some motivational book. This book is factual in its words and illustrations. Those who were victims of this kind of crime will relate well with the instances and steps stated in this book which are deployed by these online thieves in their dishonorable trade.

To the stubborn ones, those who will not bother to read this book; I pray they don't become victims before they realize the importance of this book. There is no book like this in any book-store anywhere on this planet. This is more like an inside information to the actual thing. It will take the best intelligent gathering agency reasonable amount of time and resources to get these non-fictional facts. This little book will save millions of lives and make people live better in this computer age.

Key Points

We are living in a technology driven world today. Very impressively, it has numerous advantages; the speedy passage of information from one source to another. The large communication channel this technology creates and the ability to meet and interact with people of different geographical localities. The enabling environment it creates for our businesses to thrive. There are probably a countless reasons why we should be happy about our technology driven life powered by the internet. But just like a two edged-sword it has got its bad side. There is no denial to the fact that internet has brought an equal misery and pain to man just as it has put smiles on his face. The stalking of a total stranger, cyber bully and harassment, circulation of fake information and of course internet fraud are just a few of the problems.

We shall be casting our beam of light on Internet Fraud in this book. Often than not, people are constantly losing their money to cyber thieves, gullible and mindless criminals pretending to be who they are really not. Billions of dollars are annually stolen with much of these crime cases being unsolved forever. The nature of this crime makes it very difficult to solve even by the most intelligent crime fighting institution in the world. It has taken the shape and aura of an incurable disease. It's like we are cursed by it and subsequently living with it. Many lives have been completely shattered by this art of deceit. Marriages have been broken, entire life savings of well meaning people gone into smoke and some have taken their lives as a result of the irredeemable pains and anguish brought upon them by these scammers.

It therefore becomes very important and urgent to find a solution to this plague. The wildfire is fast burning with a fierce resilience and determination. With the way it's fast spreading, every single soul might become a victim of this unfortunate misery manufactured by these unscrupulous criminals in the nearest future. Their sheer determination is like nothing else. We are possibly making a huge and costly mistake if we think that the security agencies around the world would stop this menace. They might just try to make some few arrests and prosecutions. But it's all going to be a scratch on the surface. A more holistic approach is needed to completely alienate this problem. That very approach entails that all hands must be on deck. Every single child and adult must consciously act to suppress the influence of these online robbers. I am contributing with the information I will be sharing in this book.

There is only two ways to find out if my assertions are correct or not. First, anyone who has ever been scammed will completely agree with me on the method deployed by their scammers. Secondly, those that ignore to read this book will definitely find out the truth in this book when they are scammed. By then, they would have lost one hundred times of the price of this book. You have made a wise decision in buying this book. I suggest you save others by encouraging them to buy also. They will thank you later for your kind advice. If these criminals are expanding in numbers every passing second, then we should also expand the number of those who have access to this all important book. I will make this book very simple and direct to the point. The objective is to detect and stop a possible cyber theft from occurring. Information is the key! This book is that very information! Use it!

Key Note:

Remember you cannot trust social media platforms with accountability. Most of them are so engrossed with having many users on their platforms rather than adhering to user protection rights. All they want is a platform to do Ads for their greed satisfying business agenda. Daily, they make millions of dollars in their Ads services. If they were really sincere, most of the fake profiles would be deleted from their data base. But if they do, they will lose money. Sadly, they prefer you lose your own money through scam on their platform. **You're really alone in this world. You must be your own protector.** They don't really care as much as they want to make you believe. They are so many fake accounts on most of these social media platforms. No reliable verification process to really ascertain the genuineness of information provided by users.

CHAPTER ONE

What is fraud?

Fraud is a universal crime that has no race or gender coloration. *It is human nature for man to seek undue progress through inordinate means, ways that contravene extant laws that govern the affairs of men at any given time and place.* From the beginning, the art of defrauding unsuspecting victims has been prevalent. Ever since man learnt how to keep records, such fraudulent acts can be seen on records. Even instances where man failed to keep records, tales of such ugly incidents have been told from generation to generation. It's seems the genetic makeup of mankind has fraud laced up in it. There is no form of fraud that has not occurred since the beginning of man's existence on God's green earth. Some of these acts are re-occurring in different patterns with modifications with respect to the dynamics of time and place. No society, no matter how strong it's laws and enforcement, can be bold to claim of it success in eradicating this scourge. It's like the air we breathe. We can't do without it.

I mean it when I say we all can't do without fraud. Everybody is caught up in its ugly web. It's either you are perpetuating the crime or you are unknowingly a victim. At one point in time or another we have been a victim of fraud. Most times we are caught off guard by the least people we suspect. They are usually our loved ones, most respected religious people, the sweet talking politician, etc. From experience, I can boldly declare that every single being on this planet has fallen victim of fraud at one point or another including the best fraudsters.

This crime is so hard to evade because it involves trickery, an indirect means of persuading someone or people to agree to something for the sole purpose of taking undue advantage of them without their consent. Most times when the victims find out, it's already late and the criminal is likely not there to face the consequences of their actions. Some other times, the victims are usually very stupid to convince themselves otherwise, just to avoid looking like a fool. They give reasons to justify why they have been defrauded. This is just their ego playing on their reasoning faculty.

No need to be ashamed of yourself when duped. It's of course partly your fault but just remember you are not alone. It's not about being smart or super intelligent. A "stupid" kid on the street with little or no education can con the most intelligent person in a cozy office. The number of potential con mark has more to do with the success of a well articulated con. People con millions of people at the same time almost all the time. For instance, take a look at the relationship between the political elites and the masses. History has shown that every politician is a con man.

Be it a politician in America, Europe, Africa or Asia. These people are so crafty that they have mastered the art of divide and rule. They make the masses to be at polar ends choosing between two evils. At the same time, the masses fight amongst themselves on the grounds of party affiliation and ideology. In the very end, the political class achieves their selfish goals by scamming the masses. Most naive people doing blind followership will disagree with me on this. I wouldn't blame such people because most cons are like spell. They take years for you to come to your right senses, some never leave you. You're so neck deep into it that you tend to convince yourself that it is not a con.

Once upon a time, a certain President in a powerful Nation wanted a pretext to invade a smaller Nation in the Far East. He needed the support of his people to achieve his military invasion. The accusation of the possession of certain deadly weapon was made against the leader of this small Nation who was seen as a tyrant by some of his own people and foreigners alike. In the end, after the invasion it was discovered that such weapon never existed.

The leader was later captured by this stronger Nation and with his death televised around the globe. In the end, unimaginable sums of money were spent in this military exercise. Human lives were lost on both sides. The question you should ask yourself is who supplied the weapons used in that operation? Why was the President so certain that such "dangerous weapon" existed even without proof? Why rush into war if as a sane being you know the deadly consequences of war? How did this action affect his political career? Did it act in his favor or not? How did the relatives of the service men and women who lost their lives fare? Was it a con or not? I think you can answer the questions yourself.

Another instance, there is a very popular country in Africa. This country got her independence in the 1960's. In fact, this country seems to be the hub of con men and women. The worst of them all are the political elites in that very country. Just before the dawn of the 21st century, the country wanted to transit from military rule to democratic rule. They were whole lots of good and qualified people who had no military background. Yet the political elites at that time mostly serving and retired military generals installed one of their own. They were able to sell the people with the obnoxious lie that a change of Khaki into Mufti changes a man.

Only time would expose their grand con. Like they say "you can take a man from the barracks but taking the barracks out of that same man becomes a problem" He assumed total control of everything and ruled like a soldier. No one dared second guessed his directives. He became a god unto himself and everybody. At the mention of his name aroused fear amongst his political enemies. During his reign, the constitution stipulated two terms, he nearly amended the laws of the land to enable him run for third term. The same sit-tight in office that characterized the military rule that was exactly what he almost replicated in a democratic setting. Did you see the con?

A successful fraud plays with the emotions and perception of its victims. Since the people perceived everyone in khaki uniform as a bad ruler, they brought a retired General and gave him some fine civilian clothes to change the perception of the poor masses. For the fact this same man was once imprisoned for protesting against his despotic colleague's style of ruthless military fiat. They played on the people's emotions by all these. In the end, the people thought they were making the change and progress without knowing they were all scammed.

Time went by and some realized the democracy they thought they were practicing was actually a demonstration of craze. The political elites who were mostly in the military were living and breathing fat, while the larger populace starved to death with deteriorating well being in all facets of livelihood. In actual sense, they were no clear distinction between the old and the new. The only difference was that the old was code named military rule while the new was called democratic rule, democracy that only existed on paper.

In the same country, its constitution was written by some group of military people under the supervision of the worst corrupt military ruler on earth, someone who looted the country to penury. Yet this same constitution is been used in democratic dispensation. How do you marry the two? Military men writing laws for democratic rule, how can one write the basics of practice of what they don't practice? It's like Lucifer writing the Bible for God's people to read and obey the tenets in it. The same constitution reads in its beginning "We the people of this country wrote this constitution" Big fraud! The people were never consulted to make their input during the process of writing and compiling the said constitution. In order to defraud the people, the constitution has corruption imbedded in it.

So many conflicting laws can be seen in practically every page of that very constitution. For instance, the constitution allows the payment of some elected officials two thousand dollars as salaries and still makes provisions of three million dollars in what it calls "Security Vote". These officials are not saddled with the responsibility of paying any security agent. Yet the same constitution allows them to spend it at their own discretion. The money is absolutely unaccounted for. It's a big con for the same constitution to fight against corrupt practices when it is deep in corruption in its letters and spirit.

This is just one example out of many around the globe. Most governments are nothing but con establishments with the hidden agenda of defrauding the unsuspecting masses. The litany of campaign promises that are never kept when elections are won. It is a scam to hoodwink people through fine words to vote for you with no intention of fulfilling such promises. They tell you it's a democratically elected government. Democracy being the concept of rule that gives people power to determine who governs them makes majority of us to be perpetually scammed into believing we are actually in charge.

You vote for your choice candidate in every election but what informed your choice? Was it based on news or paid adverts by news outlets you so much trust? Was it based on analysis of some acclaimed infallible political analysts who are probably on the pay roll of some self serving politicians? How well is your interest represented during the policy making and executions? Why do opposing political elites always find a way to resolve their differences?

Some of them meet secretly for dinner while you keep fighting and abusing each other on behalf of politicians you support. Why do their children hardly engage in the everyday political arguments that end with no winner or loser? You are being conned everyday without knowing. I will not be surprised if you don't agree with what I just said. ***Remember, a successful con makes you form theories to defend your stupidity.***

What about faith based organizations? You think they are excluded from this human tendency of defrauding people? You must think again. Just as Karl Marx rightly said "Religion is the opium of the masses" most of us are high in our blind followership that we miss to read the clear signs all the time. We are conned by the least people we suspect. ***And a good con appears more real than the actual thing.*** I have seen situations where people buy fake

15

products because the fake product is looking more enticing than the original. Even when you want to convince them to buy the genuine product they think you want to cheat them, that's how con works. Like I said earlier, victims are usually eager to defend their stupidity.

If you are a religious bigot, believe me if I tell you have been conned by what you earnestly believed to be eternally true and correct. First, religion is faith based. Faith has to do with accepting whole heatedly in the unseen. Then how do you make conclusions of the existence of something if there is no mechanical proof of sight? I think I am beginning to sound like an atheist to some of you. But let's even get the concept of religion alright. Religion is simply set of rules designed to make man act and behave well morally and spiritually for the utmost reward of Paradise/Heaven after our journey in our mortal body.

These tenets tend to define God in one certain way or another, with each religion at variance with others in their tenets. We must agree that no dogma of any religion fell from the sky. People wrote these things no matter how holy and righteous they are or were perceived to be. Man remains fallible and prone to unimaginable high degrees of mistakes. Some said they were inspired by God to write these Holy Books. The big question is why do we have one God that will inspire different religions to follow different ways to reach him and do his will? Why this enmity between people of various religions? Is it part of God's plan to kill each other in his name? Are we just part of a grand con by some people who want control over the affairs of men?

Power mongers, who are willing to take their quest to the obscene level of playing god. Why do faith organizations still hold sway in determining who becomes a political leader even when it's obvious that politicians are con men? Most of these religious leaders are stupendously wealthy leaving a large chunk of their followers impoverished. Why do they amass such wealth, building paradise/heaven on earth while the Holy Books they preach promise us of Paradise/Heaven life after death?

Con is basically saying one thing and doing something opposite; misdirection! They preach for you to leave your security in the hands of God while they parade with mortal security men armed to the teeth. They want you to be fearless but they shy away from reprimanding murderous political leaders. You still think religion is not a con? Show me one politician that has committed heinous crimes against his people and I will show a religious man who occupies a high position in the gathering of worshippers. The signs are just obvious; people are taking advantage of man's quest for spiritual guidance. It is nothing but a scam!

You see supposed dignified institutions dishing out awards to corrupt individuals. Making them look honorable when their ways are despicably dishonorable. In so doing, they scam the people into believing that such bad elements are good. This is nothing but a con to further promote the selfish interest which could be political, of such crime personified elements in the society. How about degree awarding institutions collecting large sums of money to award degrees to persons that have no knowledge of how the institution looks like? They just send someone to take care of the shambolic process for them.

Never physically visiting and even when they do visit is not to learn. All these are crimes that have continued to bedevil man and his existence on Earth. Some sites would charge you a certain amount for a service they render in a specified period of time, only for them to secretly add the option of automatic renewal at the expiration of the subscribed period. Since this fraudulent option is embedded in such a way that the subscriber will never detect it, such companies keep deducting money from one's account. It's only when you notice that, before you can make efforts to stop such scam. Most times is usually late.

What about co-operate fraud by co-operate bodies, manufacturers of products that are advertised of doing one particular thing just to entice innocent people to buy them. Goods that are toxic when consumed but look great in their fine packages. Some cars have certain protective specifications on paper, only to be lacking when accident occurs. That drug that claims to increase or enhance your organ which most times decrease or makes it worse. Are these things not scamming? How often does the system protect the consumers?

When some pharmaceutical companies make huge donations to universities for their researches how will they expose the negative impact of their products? So many fraudulent activities in the co-operate world despite the existence of supposed laws to check-mate such dubious actions, there seems to be no remedy. That's why I said we all are caught up in this ugly web of fraud. You can't completely dodge from it.

The best you could do is to stay alert and spot them at early stage to avoid becoming a victim. This book is a compilation of actual fraudulent tactics deployed by experts in the shameful business of internet fraud. We shall restrict from calling names because this is educational material not judgmental material. The book is written to save millions of innocent people from unscrupulous people. We shall be going direct in telling you step by step of con moves used by mostly online thieves.

CHAPTER TWO

Military

We shall be dealing with a kind of scam that has to do with the military. In this very con, the criminal is posing to be a military man or woman. For this scam to be successful, there are five stages used by these criminals.

First stage

The criminal sets up a profile on any of the social media platforms. Some might even go to an online dating site. To create a convincing fake but real looking profile they source for pictures from the real profile of someone in the military who matches the personality they intend to assume. These pictures are easily gotten from Facebook and Instagram. I am sure some people will be asking how possible it is for someone to copy someone's pictures on Instagram. But there are actually free Apps that enable one to do that at the snap of a finger.

In order to make the account look more real they use V.P.N or R.D.P to mask their actual location and project their desired location. Let's assume the person's intention is to scam facebook users, the fake profile is created on facebook with the help of the V.P.N, and the scammer's profile will be displaying the masked or virtual location. This is to deceive unsuspecting victims.

Second stage

This stage is where the criminal goes in search for innocent victims. What the con man does is to choose a country of his potential targets and he looks for ways of finding real people in that very country. There is no better place to find his mark than the pages belonging to media houses of such country. He joins the page, likes their news and comments on them also. All these are to create the impression he or she is from that very country and that the news also affect him. From the comments sections, they begin to like other people's comments. Then, they start adding and following them as friends.

Third Stage

This stage is more or less the major part of the scam process. It is the familiarizing part. At this stage, the criminal creates a good touching story to lure his/her mark to become attached and continue in good talking terms with them. Since most of these social media platforms allow people to view the biography of others, it is a veritable tool in the hands of these scammers. If for instance their potential victim is a widow, they create the storyline that will meet the cravings of that lonely widow, a very good false story that will make their mark fall in love as quickly as possible.

Stage Four

In this very stage, the criminal tries to be all caring and loving, constantly texting and chatting with their victims. They do things that they know their victims desperately need but are lacking in their lives. They try to fill the void their victim's past or ex spouse left. The victim will naturally begin to fall quickly in love

Stage Five

This stage is where the victim is billed. From several days, weeks and months of chat, there is every tendency the victim has revealed so much to assist the scammer weigh their financial strength. This will help them bill the victim on an amount that they will hardly say no to. They will usually start small. Once the victim makes the first payment, the second and subsequent payments become easy. Before he or she realizes, they are already borrowing.

HOW THEY DO IT

First, they need to create an email address with the desired name they want the fake profile to bear. They can create the email address on email platforms that offer domain names that correspond with the country they want the profile to impersonate. For instance; @usa.com or co.uk. They are really very careful in choosing the right name to really match what they want to do. Then they create a Facebook account or Twitter account. Before then, they need series of pictures of someone to act as their scam profile.

Instagram provides the best place for them to go in search for people in the military of the country they want. They look for some military guy who is always posting pictures and videos. Then download these pictures and videos. They use the pictures in creating their scam social media profile on any social media platform or dating site. They would also need to set up the profile to be really convincing. They Google information on the code of conduct of the country's military they are using. Their scam profile bio must reflect these things. Like their place of birth, location and education backgrounds. These details are vital for social media platforms that require them. Their potential victims most times will go to their profile to cross check the information before trusting them. They need to make their profile look really convincing.

They would also need a V.P.N or R.D.P in a social media site that is strict on location detection. Some of them really want their I.P to match with the location they selected while setting up a profile account. But a free V.P.N can easily take care of that problem for these scammers. Some very strict dating sites really require paid V.P.N. They just need to pay for it because it's nothing compared to what they stand to gain once they have successfully scammed anybody. They would ON the V.P.N or R.D.P to avoid their account from been deleted from such platforms.

But if peradventure their profile is deleted because of this and they have any other means of communicating with their victims, they just tell you their superior in the military asked them to deactivate their social media accounts because of security reasons. So it's always vital and helpful for them to ask their victims for any other means of communicating with them like email address or phone number or social media sites which are less strict. This is to avoid losing contact with their victim in the event of this kind of eventuality.

While their profile on this social media is set up, the next task is sourcing for potential victims. Since their main objective is to scam, they need to look out for well to do individuals. If they are posing as a military man, their best preys are single working or retired ladies and divorced working or retired women. Another group is some really fat ladies who they know don't feel good about themselves. They are constantly suffering from low self esteem. Such people will easily fall for their scheming when provided with the love they so desire. The single and divorced ladies who are also very in dire need of love. They crave for fantasy which their ex never really fulfilled. They are more prone to fall head over heel when these con artists show them love and care.

In order to get these people, they go to pages, groups and platforms of country they wish to choose their victims from. They would like such pages, join such groups and platforms. Look at the comment sections and go through peoples comments. From their comments, they will deduce who is a potential mark. If she is lonely they will know from her response to issues. If she is suffering from low self esteem, they will also find out from how she responds to issues. The idea is to find the need she desperately needs and satisfy them. By so doing she will have little or no reason to suspect them. Before she realizes what's happening she is already paying them with her life savings. News channel pages are also a very good tool used by these scammers in sourcing for victims.

In other to get the attention of their mark, they need to also comment on their profile. Positive and heartwarming comments that will create the impression they really care. They sustain the tempo for some days. Get her to notice how kind they are with words on her profile. They will proceed to directly messaging her depending on the nature of the social platform. They can start by richly and extensively complimenting her looks even if she looked ugly to them and doesn't appeal to them. But hey! They are there for business and besides they are using someone else's picture. All they want is to get her to fall for the person they are impersonating.

They don't come out too forward to announce their intentions. They start really slow and steady by constantly checking up on her by chatting her up. This requires they stay online as long as possible to know when she is online. This actually will entail them staying awake at nights when her time zone is hours different. But it's just a small price to pay for what they are looking for.

They really need to study things about the country they claim to be from. Things like the kind of food people eat, leisure, sports and all others things that are peculiar to that very location. This is to enable them sound really more real to avoid suspicion from her. They need to avoid every form of slip up that will result to the failure of the scam process.

Since they are filling in the gap in her love life, a time will come when she will want more than just chats on the social media platform. She will likely ask for a phone number, email address etc. Even if she doesn't ask, they can always be the first to do so. Because of this they need to be prepared long before hand. Since they are not from the country they claim to be from, getting a mobile number seems to be difficult for amateurs. But it is not for those that know the right place to look for it. They can easily download Apps on Play Store or Apple Store that renders mobile phone service with the number of their country choice by just using the internet. By so doing they have what looks like a real phone number of such country. Some of these Apps allow them to text and call that very country unlimited with calls to other countries coming with charges. They also need a V.P.N or R.D.P to mask their location while using the App so as to trick the application that they are in that very country.

If they cannot find any free calling App, they are cheap paid similar Apps that gives them exactly what they need. Such paid lines allow them to even create a WhatsApp profile with it. We all know how credible the WhatsApp platform is in validating real phone numbers. With such number and functional

WhatsApp, it becomes absolutely impossible for their victims to suspect them. With this they maintain a constant communication with her which will create the impression they really care about her. They will be the first to wake her up with really good message, routinely sending her some inspirational messages to uplift her spirit. She is probably lonely and all these will make her really feel loved and cared for.

Since they told her they are serving in the military, the victim might start asking them questions regarding the military. They really do need to gather as much information about the military of that country. It's always easy for them to lie to be serving in a war torn region. Middle East is their best destination, with Syria being a very good decor. So they need to know more about Syria if they were using the country.

They need to know practically everything about the ongoing Syria war, the causes, players, casualties and daily update of the conflict. They also need to know their time zone and probably save it in their mobile phone because the victim is bound to regularly ask them what time it is in the place they pretend to be. In such moments they don't need to flutter or waste a second. They practically pattern and organize their daily activities to reflect the time zone of Syria or any other conflict zone they might choose to work with.

Since they are always online chatting and texting her. She is probably going to ask them why they spent so much time online with her. She is going to doubt if they actually go to the battle field at all. As a soldier in conflict region they are claiming to be, they are required to fight on the battle ground once in awhile. In order to maintain their cover, they will usually tell her they are in the communication units and as such hardly go to the battle field.

The closest they get to the field is during a weekly patrol which usually lasts for some couple of hours. This very lie is just to make her feel relaxed and expect more caring and loving through regular chats and calls. They know she is in dire need of companionship and their duty in this con is to provide her with that. If they are too good in doing so, she will most likely not accept any advances from other men, even those she is physically seeing. She is going to trust them, a total stranger more than anyone else.

Since they downloaded pictures and videos from the Instagram page of someone they are posing as, it's necessary for them to always post different pictures once in awhile. This is to make them look more legit. No one trusts a total stranger who has only one picture. They need to look alive! If they have videos, they post them too, never giving her reasons to doubt their actual existence. The victim might have probably told the con man about her life. Things like her family members and love life. It is just right for him to also find a cover story to portray himself in exactly what will appeal to her.

He could just tell her that his wife divorced him or she died a few years back and left him with a kid. That he is a very lonely man in a lonely job. He was using the advantage of serving in the communication unit of the Army to find true love online. They will also download the picture of a random lady and child to match the story that their wife is late or separated. Such pictures will arouse pity which will ultimately lead to some kind of love. Human beings are wired to feel love for the weak even when that weakness is faked. All she is seeing is an emotionally weak and lonely man, coupled with her boring and lonely life; she is bound to fall for the whole tailored story.

In their phone call conversation, she might notice an accent that is quite different from the country they are claiming to be from. They will quickly allay her fears by telling her that they have double citizenship. Making up a story of how one of their parents is from a different part of the World. Telling her how they spent most of their life in such place and only recently moved to the country where they are claiming to be from and got enlisted in the military. With this very convincing story she will relax and continue in the affair.

If she persists and doesn't buy into the story, they try to play the victim by telling her how they felt disappointed in her for the lack of trust, making her feel the pain of doing wrong to an innocent man. They are clever not to over play it! They can even end the call on her and pretend to be angry with her. They will not call or return her calls for some days. If she texts them, they don't reply. If she sends message to them on any social media platform, they don't respond. This will further break her down. She is going to become afraid of losing him, the one thing that has brought her love and care. When she has apologized enough, they will resume communications with her. They don't talk about that very problem again. If they do, they are going to open an old injury. In some cases, they are most likely going to be on the begging side. They just move on as though nothing happened.

If she ever asks for a video chat, they will tell her the gadget used in the military doesn't support video chat. If she is persuading them to find a means to make that happen, they tell her they would be dismissed if they are caught doing so; that such act amounts to a grave security risks to their unit. If she has limited or zero knowledge about the military, she is most likely going to ask friends or relatives at some point about all that the con man has told her about the military. These relatives or friends could probably discredit the scammer's story and encourage her to stop whatever they had going on.

Her final decision is largely dependent on the thief. How well was their story? How caring and loving they have been to her. Because of this, it's really vital they maintain a close and constant communication with her. They must know special dates in her life like birthdays. If her birthday was to come up within the period of the whole con, they need to really send a beautiful message to her. If she was their only mark on that very social media account, they will put her picture and publicly celebrate her. If they had other potential victims on their friend list, it becomes counterproductive to do so. In such case, they send their eulogies secretly through private inbox. If they could afford to send her a card or gift, they will do so. Such gesture will really cast away every little shred of doubts about their genuineness.

It sounds difficult to send such gifts to her since they are not from the country she is residence at. They don't use their real name and card details to buy such gifts in online stores. They also do not want her to see their

33

name as the sender when the delivery man delivers the birthday present to her doorstep. At this point, a co-conspirator resident in that country comes into play. It will shock you to know that they are so many people that are willing to assist these con men in this ignominious act.

All they need is some level of trust and he or she can easily agree to work with them in the con process. The scammers will send the money to their partner in crime. Double of the actual price of the gift or item they intend to buy for their mark. The co-conspirator takes the remaining balance as their pay for the job they will execute. All they do is to tell their mark that someone they know back home will be assisting them in sending her the gift. It is so because they cannot access their money from their duty post because of the location they were serving as military men.

The last stage is the billing, the pay day for the con man. The time it takes to arrive at this point is dependent on the mark. Some are very stubborn and hardly fall for the con man's lies and made-up stories. If she has been hurt in the past by a lover it becomes more difficult for the con artist to get paid. And also, if she knows anyone that has been scammed with similar story the scammer has been telling her, it also make their task more tedious. But if all these obstacles don't manifest, it becomes easier for them to get to their pay day quicker than expected.

All in all, they are usually very patient, waiting for the pay day to arrive no matter how long it takes. When it finally does and they are certain that their mark will not reject their billing. Without wasting any further time; they will bill her. They will most times start with really small amount. Most times big amount will scare her and reveal the iron hand masked in a velvet glove. They can tell her they wish to transfer their next of kin to her. This will create the impression she is the most trusted and closest person in the con man's life at that point in time. They don't mention about money at first. They will allow her react to the proposal. She is most definitely going to subtly turn the offer down. But they will persist and give her reasons why she needs to accept to be their next of kin. Citing the love and relationship the two have had over the period of time as the reason why she needs to be their next of kin. If she finally accepts it, which in most cases she will. They will request that she email to them her details.

Details like full names, address, occupation, place of work, relevant identification card and phone number. Telling her they will be mailing those details to the appropriate quarter in the military for the processing of the change of next of kin. At this point, they create an email address that resembles an official military email address of that very country. They will customize an email with the military logo and headings to convince her it was coming from the official source. In that message they will inform her that the military board has received a message on the change of next of kin from the person they are impersonating to be. They will inform her to respond to this message to confirm if actually she was aware of it. They are usually very meticulous to avoid any form of mistakes in spellings. Their tenses usually look official and direct to the point.

If she responds to the message, then they will bill her by telling her it will cost her money to effect this change. The scammer tries to be less greedy. They let the amount reflect what she can easily afford without asking people to borrow her money. In most cases, her money lenders will counsel her against making such payment. They scammers try to avoid pushing her to a third party. If she is willing to pay which most likely, she will message the scammer of the latest development.

He acts really concerned and convinces her he would have given her the money if he could access his bank account. He assures her of his readiness to pay her back, once he comes back from the war zone. They really sound very real at this point. When she accepts to foot the bill, the payment detail of their co-conspirator in her country is given to her to make the payment. They convince her through the fake official military email address they proposed she paid through an individual to ease her stress in the process. The payment could be made through western union, money gram or any other pick up cash services.

Once she successfully completes the transaction, the scammer is in for a bigger pay. She has committed herself and she is bound to pay higher amount in the nearest future. They keep coming with make-believe stories that will require she assists them financially as they are unable to access their bank account. For this to be more effective, they assure her they have applied for a leave to come home which was been processed, that both of them will tie the knot once they come back. With this promise of happy life ever after, she is bound to do anything for the scammer. She can even borrow or sell her property to please the con man

CHAPTER THREE

Business/Investment

This kind of fraud is the type where some fine looking wealthy person or persons trick you into investing in a business opportunity. This opportunity is usually done online where you basically have no physical contacts with whoever that is supposedly going to manage your investment. The goal of these con men is to take as much as possible from you in your bid to make quick cash through jumbo profits.

Stage one

This is where the con man creates email accounts to enable them register their dubious social media platforms. He needs to choose a name and gender that will be suiting to the con. Depending on the country he was targeting, he will most likely use their domain to make it more convincing to the potential victims. He needs as many email accounts as possible for multiple registrations on online platforms.

Stage two

This is where the con man registers and creates profiles with email addresses he created. Since most of these social media platforms are built to be used on different browsers in one phone, it places him on advantage to operate multiple profiles at the same time. For the profiles to look real, he needs to get pictures and videos of fine dressed and rich looking people on other social media platforms. He gets as many pictures and videos as possible. He also routinely gets new pictures and videos from the wall of these people he is impersonating.

Stage three

This is where the scammer goes in a coordinated hunt for victims. He really spends time online, checking people's bio and how rich looking they are. He needs to be sure that whoever he adds to his friend list is able to invest enough money when he tells them to. To be certain he goes for rich looking people.

Stage four

At this stage he tries to play nice and friendly after he has become friends with his potential victims on the social media platforms. It could be on a dating site. But whichever one, the con man really acts all good intentional so as to gain some level of trust from their mark. He is always going to be posting pictures of good moments, adventure and pleasurable experiences. He acts as though he was really making so much while working less. Some victims while seeing all these constant posting of photos and videos get financially aroused. The urge to also live in that very fantasy being displayed by the con man sets in. They will start commenting and liking those posts. Some might even go as far as initiating the first contact through private chat.

Stage five

This is the final stage where the con man really assures his potential victims of the safety of their investment. He will act all not interested in making them join in the investment while indirectly persuading them to. He is always going to be giving them reasons why they need to join in the investment. The victims being gullible and deceived by the photos and videos fall for his trap. Just before they realize it, they are probably thousands of dollars down in their account.

HOW THEY DO IT

This very form of scam is pretty hard and requires time and fund. The con man might also need the collaboration of five other people to make it work. First they really need to know and understand what they are going into. They need to posses as much information on trading and investment as possible. They don't leave anything to chance because their potential victims will be asking them business and investment related questions. They cannot afford to fail not to give them accurate answers. At this point is where they need extra hands to pull it off. But let's even go down to how the con men go about with this kind of fraud.

They really need to create email addresses as much as ten. These email addresses are useful to them when they want to create profiles on social media platforms where their targets are. Since it is absolutely free to create such emails, it's the least of their worries. Even if they needed a paid email address that will give them a unique domain, it was relatively cheap to do so when compared to what they stand to gain. Such specific and unique domain will give them more credibility and bring this aura of trust and confidence among their victims. Such email addresses will usually bear names that will tally with the country they choose to be from. This is just in case they wanted to email their victim at any point in time during the con. The victim gets to see that everything checks in.

When they have successfully created those emails, they proceed to creating profiles on social media platforms that they so desire to scam people from. Before doing so, they really need pictures and videos of people they want to impersonate. Since they were pretending to be successful investors and business people, they really need good looking pictures and videos, like expensive looking vacation pictures. Good enticing happy moments with family. Pictures of shopping experience in a world class mall. All these are just to appear and look very wealthy. Picture they say speaks more than a thousand words.

The victims are more going to be looking at the pictures these con men post on such platforms than what they tell them. People are more deceived through what they see than what they hear. Their job is to deceive the innocent victim, so they must use these little tricks. Human nature you can call it. Getting such pictures is as easy as anything. They go to Instagram and Facebook, where there are lots of such pictures and videos. The name of the person they will use will be entirely different from the name they will be using on such platforms. It's simple, they just use a different name while copying and posting the real person's pictures and videos as the real person posts them.

Since their victims don't possibly know the real person physically, it will be difficult for them to spot the main person. Some of them will just assume is just one individual who is using different names on the same or different social media platforms. When they have successfully set up this profile, they will narrow down their search to country or countries they wish to scam people from. Most likely, they are far away from such country and might have never been there. Smart con men will choose a country where collecting money from their victim will not be a problem. They look for a country that has less economic hassle in doing international transaction with their real resident country.

They will also study the country, state and province they are faking to be from. They have to gather necessary information about such terrain. The fraudsters must know the time zone which they can easily set on their mobile phone to accurately know what time it is in such place. You might wonder why they need such little detail. Unfortunately, it is important to them in assisting them in their chat with victims. Occasionally people ask others what it is in their locality over the course of social media chat. In such a time they don't need to waste time trying to Google it. Such waste of time will amount to suspicion from victims. They don't leave anything to chance. The con man must be ready like a soldier to respond accurately to every question. So it is really needful for them to study and understand these details.

Some platforms allow users to add as many friends as possible once they Sign Up. In such case they need to start adding many friends immediately. Before that, they post so many pictures, videos and business inspiring quotes to reflect their supposed rich lifestyle. People are always going to check the profile of others to see who they are friends with on these social media platforms. It's a disaster for the con man to appear like a novice with a barren and empty profile.

He needs to make his profile look rich and enticing. Presenting the victims with a profile that will make them scroll up and down for some minutes; while being held spell bound by the captivating posts. In the case where the platform bans or blocks newly created accounts that they see adding many users, the con man will relax. Patience comes into play in such case. He needs to patiently grow in such platform by occasionally adding few people and posting rich contents on his profile. If the scammer cannot exercise the required patience, he can buy an already existing account. Are you shocked? You can easily buy 3 to 5 years old social media accounts from willing owners or hackers. Since these platforms allow you to sign up free, people create as many profiles as possible just to sell at a later date.

If the con man reaches out to such people, they are most times willing to sell at a cheap price. Something they never paid for while signing up, it will be profiting to them to sell it at a very relatively small price that will amaze you. If the con man cannot find who to buy from, stealing becomes another good option. If they care less about their close friends and family members they can without thinking twice snoop on them why they login their account. They get their password and change it to become theirs.

These friends and close associates are most likely going to suspect the con man if they knew what he was up to and in most cases they are usually not aware. If they knew the con man indulged in online scam they will discourage him because of the legal implications. When he is caught, they will suffer the shame and financial loss through hiring of lawyers and visiting him in prison. No sane person wants that for those they are close to. Once the fraudster buys or steals this account, they need to change everything about the account. They start by deleting and blocking all the existing friends and followers in that account. Then changing the name and every single detail of the account to reflect what they intend to use it for. They will subsequently start adding new friends and followers. Nobody will suspect a thing.

If they are convinced that they have gathered enough targets as followers and friends, they will to start making advances on them. But they have to put themselves in their victims' shoes. If it was them, would they believe anything someone who has the kind of profile they have says to them. If yes, they continue and if no, they have more work to do. They don't want to give the impression that they are solely on that platform to lure people into investing. They try to make it look more like they are just some regular rich person who has earned so much through investing in business opportunities.

Once they are able to pass this message across to their friends, then they are good to go. Since the con man needs evidence to the lifestyle he is showcasing, he needs collaboration. People who will like and comment on his posts. At the beginning, they don't expect their victims to do that, people are cold hearted on these platforms. Some of them are just very suspicious of everything and everyone. They are definitely not going to appreciate the scammer's posts. So he needs collaborating profiles to do that. These profiles can be simultaneously operated by him or his partners in crime. This is to like, retweet, share and comment on his posts. With that they are lending credence to the credibility of his fake profile.

These collaborating profiles must be generous with praise when needed. If it requires them validating a point the con man raised concerning investment, they must also be quick to concur with him. With all these, his potential victims will join his other profiles to praise and worship his elegance. People like to join the winning team. Nobody likes a lonely soul. They want a taste of the piece of cake. To them those profiles praising the con man are real.

When he starts noticing this, the scammers will return the favor also to his victims. He likes, shares, comments and retweets their posts. By so doing, the scammers are creating an impression that they care and appreciate the victims too. This is to water the ground for them when they finally approach the victim in direct and private message. When they do, they don't go direct into announcing their intentions. At first, the con man cultivates that casual friendship seed. He will chat with them about their private lives if they are open and receptive to his advances. In most cases, they are usually open. Who doesn't like a rich and wealthy man or woman? Human instinct allows people to accept and associates with folks they are mostly like going to benefit from.

This very truth will act and work in the con man's favor. But he doesn't feel too comfortable about this. He must really study each person to know exactly what they are like and the best way to approach them individually. If they are lonely and need love, he satisfies their fantasy by showing them love. If they are religious, he becomes pious in his communications with them. If they hold a certain political view, he aligns also with them in their political views. The con man makes the conversation all about his mark. He fills in the void and space in their life, being their source of inspiration. With that, trusting him becomes as easy as the word easy sounds.

When he gains their trust, he proceeds to talking about himself. He creates a really good story to trap them in his cobweb of deceit. Each person might require the con man creating a unique story about him. What Mr. A believes will not make Mr. B to believe too. So he needs to learn and put into consideration the individuality of each of his potential victim. He tells them good stories of his success in the business/investment world; a story that makes him sound too confidence about his investment strategies.

He will usually give them the possible risks involved and at the same time allay their fears by giving them clues to navigate such risks. Clues and tactics the victims believed to be used by the con man. He makes them understand that fear of losing their money is quite natural, as him felt the same way at the beginning. It took courage for him to go pass that monstrous obstacle called fear and today he was glad he did so.

He doesn't pressure them about investing. He tries to refrain from completely making their conversations about business and investment even when he feels they trust him. The scammers talk about other things while indirectly luring his potential victims into bringing up business related topics. When his victims fall for that trap, they don't hesitate to preach their gospel in a whole new dimension.

The con men can always cite their recent investment success. While surreptitiously convincing their mark by posting and talking about the success of those they brought into the investment world. Their collaborating profiles will be at hand to agree and concur with them. These other profiles will comment and thank him for his assistance. All these things will be seen by his victims and in no distant time his innocent victims will be all out to invest in the platform which was been controlled by him and his criminal associates. He appears more real by advising them to start with small amount to avoid losing big. This singular counsel will make his marks to believe in the lie that he actually care for them. The idea is to convince them to give it a trial.

This investment could be either a group or page created on Facebook with members investing to get a certain profit at the end of a stipulated period. The majority of people on this kind of group are collaborators in the scheme or simply accounts controlled by the scammers. They will regularly give testimonies of how they earned or made fat profits from the scheme. When they finally add their victims, these unsuspecting victims will be more convinced by the made up testimonies from already existing members of the group. Most times the scammers can ask them to join on their own by giving them the link to the page. They even screenshot manipulated bank account balance to further entice these people.

The con men are really smart to spell explicitly how the group functions. Things like the least and highest amount an investor can make at a given time. The means of investing, it could be bank wire to the central account or cash pick up services. They can even suggest crypto currency to their victims. But they don't make it compulsory to their victims to invest through coin as this will spook them. People are more comfortable with bank wire and money transfer as they feel they can always lodge in complaint at their financial institution if anything goes wrong. In crypto currency, there is no one to complain to. Even when one complains, it is almost impossible to trace the thief.

The scammers have to silently pray their victims opt for the crypto currency. This will benefit them more. If they choose all other means they will have to share their loot with a co-conspirator resident in the same country with the victim. As bad as it may seem, it's a necessary thing to do in order to maintain their cover and tracks. Their first priority is to have their identity hidden. As a con man that was just starting in this scheme, he needs to build genuine confidence. I mean real confidence by paying out to his first few victims. It sounds absurd right? You are probably wondering why the scammers need to pay out their victims when the actual aim of the whole scheme is to defraud them. But it's the wisest thing to do as professional con artists.

Their aim is to hit the big jackpot. They need the lion share not some meager money that can barely cover the expenses they have put in to make it work. Once they pay the real victims, such people will not hesitate to broadcast the good news to more people. They will tell their colleagues in their work place and family members too. These victims will make the work of the thief easier by unknowingly playing the devil's advocate. Even those that doubted them prior to their decision to invest in such platform will be very eager to invest now. Seeing they say is, believing. They can now see the profits made by the person who they know physically and trusts. In a short period of time, the platform will be so crowded by victims who other victims brought.

In some cases where the scammer doesn't have enough money to pay, he might even resort to borrowing. The risk is worth taking. In fact it is unavoidable for the con men not to put in their personal money. Let's assume their investment platform is promising 100% profits at the end of one week of investment. And out of the money the victim invested their oversea collaborator has taken like 30% of the money invested. This is his cut for receiving the money for them. He serves as a middle man between them and their victim.

He brings the trust in the whole scheme. So after one week as promised the scammers need to come up with 130% of that money to pay to the victim. As painful as it may appear, they need to do that if they are actually looking for the bigger piece of the meat. But if they were just out for the small things, they can pocket the money and not pay back, which means they needed to spend more time convincing new people to join. While doing so, they will also pray that those that invested who they didn't pay don't contact their potential victims.

They will spoil the show for the con men by telling these victims about their ordeals with the platform. To keep such gatecrashers at bay, they need to delete and block them from their social media accounts and make sure they have no access to comment on their posts ever. If they do, like some will create a new account to come for revenge or probably try to warn others. Then the scammers are bound to lose. Most times they will start reporting to the online platform about the ongoing scam. If that happens, the scammers need to start afresh by creating new profiles and starting up another similar scheme with entirely new names and pictures. The best in this game knows it's far better to allow the victims to campaign for him, so as to make enough money once and for all.

If the con man has enough money, he can hire someone to create an investment website for him. With as little as $300 dollars he can actually get willing and expert web developers to set up a really good looking website that will lure even the most difficult being on earth. But if he is well knowledgeable on web development then he doesn't need to spend on building the website. To achieve that he needs to correctly and meticulously write every single letter that will be on the site to suit his con.

The paid web developer might not have the required knowledge of what he needs. Even if he does, he might probably not want to get involved in the scam. The scammer can easily give him a different write up to make it look legit. Once he is through with the work and hands him full access, he would then change things to suit his fraudulent venture.

This way is better for him in order to conceal his identity especially if he contacted and paid the web developer through means that reveals his identity. But these scammers can also contact some underground criminal minded web developers who will most likely get paid through the virtual currency. In such case they have nothing to worry about.

Since the web site is mainly targeted at victims in countries outside their own, they need to host the site in one of such choice countries. You are probably wondering how these criminals can do this. If they have a trusted co-conspirator, they can wire money to him from their country. Usually they have to wire more than double of the actual price to serve as payment for his services. He will easily host the site in his resident country with the local mobile number of that place.

In the event they don't have such person they can trust to do that for them, they can equally do it on their own. The internet is so designed in a way to reduce hassles for genuine users. But that advantage is sadly a disadvantage to the security of innocent users. All they need to do is to download a free App that assigns an international number. They also can buy one with less than $50. When they have gotten that, the scammers just need to pay with their debit or credit card from their country of residence. When filling their information, they select the country they wish to have the site hosted as their country of residence. The international number they bought will trick the system to believe they were actually in such country. The hosting company will call or text to them the confirmation using the phone number they bought. With that their site will look legit.

The domain provider will never reveal their card details making their actual location completely masked. When people check the site details, they will see the country they are pretending to be in. The paid phone number too will cement the lies. With that they are set to start looking for victims from social media platforms and dating sites. They can always give the site 3 months before bringing people to it. Some people are too careful that they will run a background check on the site.

Since they are claiming to have been paying people in their investment site, they need some couple of months old site to validate that lie. Just as in the page scenario, they can always pay the first few victims to lure more to the site. The paid international number will serve as the website contact line. They need to be fluent in English or any other language that is the official language of the country their site is hosted. If the scammer is a man, he deems it necessary to recruit a female collaborator to act as customer care agent. Females are least suspected when it comes to crime. But if he must do it as a man, he will be gentle and caring with words. He needs to master the excellent customer care services to attend to his victims. Most of the victims will first call to ask litany of questions before investing. Like I said previously the scammers need to know almost everything about investment.

The site could also be built to trade with crypto currency. This will remove the need to have somebody get their cut when they assist him in receiving or sending money from or to his victims. To add more credibility to the site, the scammers usually upload official documents showing their company name is registered with the appropriate financial regulatory commission. To a novice it sounds difficult to do since their site is nothing but a scam site. Who would in their right senses give them these documents? But they don't need no one's permission or authority to do that. All they need is to find similar legit site like their own. Such legit sites most times upload such documents on their home page for convincing purposes. He can use that to his own advantage by copying or downloading it. With the necessary App, they can easily edit it by replacing the original details with their own.

Exposing internet fraudsters

CHAPTER FOUR

Online Dating

This is very common on almost all the social media platforms. Over the years some people have even gone ahead to create a unique platform specifically for that purpose. Such platforms are abound and commonly referred as dating sites. They are so many of them on the internet, offering free or premium package. The number of people on such sites is just mind blowing and the numbers keep increasing.

First stage

These online thieves need to create an email address, which is more like the ABCD of every form of internet communications. With this, they can access and sign up on any social media platforms, dating sites inclusive.

Second stage

This is the stage where they go in hunt for potential victims. In order to achieve this, these scammers need convincing profiles on these online platforms, with really good looking and enticing pictures. Videos too are regularly uploaded by these unscrupulous people.

Third stage

This is where they make contact by directly messaging their victims on these platforms. They really play nice and all caring. They try to get you to fall in love with them.

Fourth stage

At this final stage is where they bill their innocent victims. They do this by coming up with all kinds of story that requires financial assistance. This is where they milk you dry if you are not careful.

HOW THEY DO IT.

This very form of scam requires so much from the scammer in terms of time because he is going to be in people's lives. He has to be online steady to always chat with his victims and respond to their messages. He becomes ultimately their source of joy; he must be available to live up to it. He is usually prepared. For a start, he needs to create an email account with the name, age and gender of who he chooses to impersonate. He could still pretend to be a man even if he was really a woman or vice versa. But since women are rare in this line of work, mostly it is men pretending to be women.

Men can also pretend to be other men with corresponding name and race. They need to choose wisely on which one suits their capability. They have to create that email address to reflect all these things. They have to make sure the names tally with what they will use on the social media platforms. This is just in case if their victims want to write them through email. It's amateur for these scammers to give their email address that doesn't tally with their name. They are very careful at this stage because it's the foundation which will determine their success or failure. Using a password they could always remain is also vital. As trivia as it seem, it's really important to them.

The next stage is for them to move on to any social media platform. But just before they do so, they need pictures and videos of someone they will be impersonating. The person must really look good and attractive. It's dating, so they need to appear charming and sexy. All they need to do is to spend really good quality time on Facebook or Instagram to search for individuals who are constantly posting their pictures. With the help of some App they can download the pictures and videos seamlessly. These scammers avoid individuals that are popular like celebrities.

They cannot impersonate such people for long without running into their fans. The scheme will fail when they use such people even in the most secret and relatively unknown websites. The online thieves copy as much of the persons pictures and videos as possible. This is just to avoid running into trouble if the person blocks him from viewing their profile. To be on the safe side, they don't comment on such people's posts to avoid provoking them. They are just their silent friend or follower. With this, the scammer can always have access to copy their pictures at the least possible suspicion from such people.

Daily and regularly they have to make their fake profile look real by uploading those impersonating materials. They are careful not to over post such materials to avoid looking desperate. They don't have to post too many pictures at once. No one does that kind of thing. Such acts are not good in the crime world. The scammer has to compliment the photos/videos with good posts of really crafted inspiring sentences. The fraudster posts about his daily activities, family and things happening around the world. They live and embody the life of that person they are impersonating.

They replicate exactly what the person could be doing on the daily by using their pictures to make these conjectures. If the scammer cannot imagine and come up with this idea, then they copy the lifestyle of that person if it suits their plan. But usually it doesn't, because the real person is living a true life and probably not interested in wooing people into online dating. On the other hand the scammer was solely on the online platform for making people fall in love with him. So, its best they come up with their own style while at the same time using the person's pictures and videos. They also refrain from using posts that contain specificity with locations.

The professional con men never use the same location as the person they are impersonating. It will be easier for people to catch them; it could be their friends, relations or them personally. And while posting their pictures, the con man is very observant to study the picture very well. The background can expose his lie. For instance; if he was claiming to be in London and in the picture of the person, there is a Las Vegas street number or symbol. With this, people can easily detect and find out he is lying. Even in the videos he will be posting, he is also really careful.

They don't post a video of someone they are impersonating carrying out a surgery as a surgeon while on their fake profile they claim to be an engineer. Or posting a picture with rivers/water in the background when their fake profile says they live in a desert-like region. All these little slip-ups will expose them instantly. Some people are fond of sniffing around, they will spot such discrepancies.

While taking into cognizance of these details, the scammer knows he is also required to be careful with the kind of people he adds as his friends on these social media platforms. There are so many people who are also there with the same objective as him. He is there to scam others and can't scam his kind. It could be likened to a snake trying to swallow its kind. And these fake accounts of his kind will also put the scammer in trouble, especially if they are controlled by amateur con men.

The system will easily block and blacklist them when people complain about them, which most likely it's possible. When this happens and they form a greater percentage of his friend list, he is definitely going to taste their misery. It's like mingling with the unhappy. It was just a matter of time before you become sad and depressed like them too. A professional con man avoids such people as much as he can. It's easy to do so, since he already knows how a con man behaves. Once they reflect his fake and impersonating style, he cuts them off or never accepts them in the first place. To be on the safer side, he would usually go through their profile before requesting or accepting to be their friend on those social media platforms.

As he is screening to avoid his kind, he is also keen to select those that will easily fall for his scheming. Let's assume he was acting to be a lady, his focus would be on men, single or divorced. There are so many men on the internet who are solely there to cheat on their wife. He could be lucky to find such people, they are usually easier to con. The scammer presents them with the fantasy they are desperately craving for. He spots such people through their profile. He checks if it says married, how often they post things about their marriage. Such men don't usually talk about their wife or kids. If he monitors them very well, he will notice their marital misery which is reflected on their social media lifestyle. The way such men comment on posts and their opinions on issues relating to marriage and family. As little and irrelevant it may sound, it's actually very important to his success or failure.

So he scrolls through their profiles before sending them friend request or following them. He doesn't have to waste his time on unproductive victims. Then for the single men, the scammer is very careful to select those that he feels could be ready or mostly interested in marriage. He avoids men who are always posting pictures of where they are in the company of beautiful women. Such men have real life sexual happiness and will be extremely difficult to have them fall for his trick. The con man targets the single men who are somewhat shy and look unhappy. Those who are always posting work related things.

Chances are they don't have love life and will be prone to fall into his trap easily. Another people in his radar are the widowers. Not those that their spouse recently died. Such people are difficult for the scammer to scam. They are most likely still moaning and will not have that time to start listening to him. But if he chooses to go after them, it could actually act in his favor. He plays and acts nice towards them, living in their misery with them. If possible he acts more touched and pained than the bereaved. He becomes their shoulder they will cry on and that person to lean on in their moaning moment. When they are completely healed and they don't have a lady in their life, they will fall for the scammer.

He also goes after older and fat looking men, men who are easily rejected by young girls in real life. Most of them are on the internet to try their luck. Chances are they have witnessed multiple and endless disappointments from women. Some of them too might just be sexual perverts with high libido. Men who are in desperate need of who to satisfy their animalistic urge with. From the scammer's fake sexy and good looking pictures and videos, they will easily believe her to be real because they are not thinking straight. The con man is quick to add and accept people like that.

He concentrates on adding many of them, they are his potential victims. While adding them he is smart not to over add them at once. Bit by bit, in order not to arouse security suspicion from the website. The online platform is most likely going to block his account if they noticed the unusual adding of people. So he is patient and takes it slow. He understands that the world belongs to the patient man. Most times he comments and likes their post instead of adding them. Some will be moved to add him because of his comments especially when he praises or aligns himself with their opinion. In so doing, they are creating that aura of genuineness for his fake profile. This will also trick the security measures put in place by the platform.

When he finally becomes friends or start following them, he is never too quick to start conversations with them. Since he was pretending to be a lady, they will come for her. Men see themselves as hunters in the game of sexual adventures. So he leaves them to make the first contact. But he makes frantic efforts for them to notice him. He is continuously being on their face, posting good and enticing pictures and things. He responds to their comments with cheerfulness, adopting the customer service or waitress approach. Being graceful in her words as a lady he pretends to be. Giving off the impression, she is up for grasp. Most of the people who are going to fall victim are mostly shy people.

They need that reassurance that they will succeed if they approached her. They could have likely failed multiple times in the past in their love life. So they need that good motivation to boast their confidence level. The scammer tries to give them all these without looking desperate of wanting a man. If they suspect this, chances are they will avoid him. Some will look at him as a scam he is. Others that would want a serious relationship with him will back trace their steps. Nobody really wants a desperate woman. She appears happy and comfortable as a single lady. From time to time he also comments on the post of those who regularly comment on his. He doesn't remain on the high horse of female ego and pride. He tries to reciprocate the love too

This will send the needed message. People are naturally drawn to those who are drawn to them. When the victims notice this, then they will waste no time in making the first contact, which the scammer is anxiously looking for. Before long, men will flood his inbox with messages. At this point he doesn't rush into accepting and giving off the impression he wants them so bad. Men value what cost them much to acquire. The con man understands not to be too quick and cheap to accept any of them. While playing on this card, he makes sure he is not too costly for them. No man wants to spend his entire time chasing after something that will cost him all he has got. Except those that are driven by the wild wind of blind love. They are just few and when they are shown little love and care by other ladies; they will opt in for them. In the end the con man becomes a loser. So he doesn't play too hard to get or too easy to get. He maintains a balance!

At first some of them will be bold to tell him in clear terms what they need. He is not going to hastily accept their proposal. Softly, he turns them down while keeping them in the friend zone. In essence, he let the whole affair be less romantic in the beginning. He avoids not playing the card of a hooker. Unless he was acting as one, then he would accept and bill them immediately.

But since he was not, he needs to bring that aura and pride of womanhood in play. Creating the impression that he was not in a hurry, but he maintains the friendship. This will give him an ample time to study the person very well and know if they are real or not. This time also will be valuable to him as they will be more eager to please and woo her. If he finally decides to open up for any of them, he doesn't publicize it by posting about it. He was on that platform for business and he needs as many "customers" as possible. Being private about it and indirectly suggests to them to keep what was going between them a secret. If not, other potential victims will take off. They need to live in the illusion that she is not taken yet. This will give him the opportunity to trap as many victims as possible in his cobweb of scam.

When he finally gets into serious commitment with them, he allows them to always start up the conversation. Letting them be on the driving seat but he must subtly control how they steer the ship in the friendship. This is typical of ladies. The scammer knows he must act that way. They are usually going to ask for other ways to reach her other than the usual chats. If the online platform allows audio or video calling, they are bound to call him. Since he is a man posing as a woman he wouldn't answer the call to prevent his victims from finding out his true identity.

He comes up with some really good excuse why he can't answer such calls. He could tell them her place of work doesn't allow workers answering calls or video calls. Some will want to find out when she is usually at home so as to call her during such free time, because no one works round the clock. In this case, he tells them but he will not come online those periods of time. This will give the impression that she is always exhausted after work and rests at home. In conclusion she doesn't have time. This is a perfect excuse for awhile.

But if things really get intense and serious, the victims will need her phone number. He is not in the place or country he claims to be, so getting their local phone number becomes the issue. But it's just simple for the experts. There are so many Apps that offer such services. Some of them are entirely free or relatively cheap. With that he can have the local phone number of any country in the world.

All he needs is a good and strong internet connection to use such numbers. Since he is a man and wouldn't want his masculine voice spoil things for him, he gets them to text him instead of calling. In the event they insist on hearing her voice he has no option than to buy a voice changer. With this tool he can twist his voice to sound feminine. When doing so, he doesn't prolong the call. He keeps it short to avoid getting caught. Such tools are usually not 100% efficient as their manufacturers want you to believe. The con man understands the importance of playing safe. If he cannot get such tools, getting a real girl to make the call is the second best option.

It will make the whole thing look real. All he needs to do is to intimate the girl what she will say and not say. If possible draft an essay, putting down word to word all she needs to say. While making such calls, he puts it on loud speaker to help monitor the call. He can easily control things by signaling her when to keep quiet and when to talk. She must really sound sexy for the sexually perverted men. Then she also sounds official and responsible for the responsible ones. In all, her voice must blend into the occasion.

If it calls for video calling and it becomes mandatory for him to do so, they are Apps that people don't know exist that will assist him. Most people know and use such Apps without knowing its full potency in the criminal world. With such Apps he can load the person's pre-recorded video and allow it to play. Then play it for few seconds and ends it. When the victims ask what happened, he is usually very quick to blame the internet connectivity.

Most times once they have seen such short video they are usually convinced that she is real. If it's a nude video, it will get the man's head popping. It's just a matter of time before they start inviting her to come visit them. When they do, he bills them flight, train or bus ticket money depending on their location and that of the place he was pretending to be at. But if they don't invite her, he can also fake a financial situation and ask for their help. It could be birthday party that she wants to celebrate, a sick parent or siblings. The scammer could even fake an accident. He just finds something that will make them succumb easily and give him the money.

Since he is not real and cannot collect the money with that very name on his fake profile. There is no valid ID or he is probably not in the same country. He needs a co-conspirator to do that for him. The scammer could always claim to be very busy and doesn't have the chance to go to the bank in the case of bank transfer or to any other money transfer outlets to cash out. Professional scammers use this person's surname as their fake surname too while setting up their profile. If they did, they could easily tell their victims that the person is their sibling. This will all make it look more real.

If not and the name doesn't match, he just tells them he/she is their trusted friend. If the victims are deeply in love and bought the scammer's fake story, nothing will stop them from paying. The con man is very careful not to over bill them. Through their conversations he must have known their financial capacity and how generous they are. He tries not to be too greedy. It's best they start paying him small money than billing them much money which will only scare them away.

However, if the scammer chose to impersonate a man, then he needs to be ready to act like a man in need of love. First, he searches on different platforms on the internet for a suitable person to impersonate. He is very careful in putting some small details into consideration. These details if neglected will spell his doom in the con venture. So he doesn't leave anything to chance. He has to consider the age, race and physical appearance. At what age would a man be and he will be easily attractive to women on the internet.

What race is easier to find women tripping for them? And the physique is also very vital too. He cannot look dull and be sexually appealing to women. He has to find that handsome man with good physique. It's not necessary he must be athletic. An average healthy looking man will fit into what the scammer is looking for. As a professional, he doesn't go impersonating someone popular. He makes sure he changes their name, location and all the details about them. All he wants is their pictures and videos.

When he has seen a good example of this, he will proceed to creating a profile on any social media platform or in an online dating site. Dating sites are usually easier and better. Their double ganger is mostly likely not on such dating platforms. If he is truly handsome, ladies in real life will flock around him so much that he will hardly have extra time to look for love on the internet. This will act in the con man's favor by making sure his cover doesn't get blown.

Because if the person were to see that someone was using his pictures on a different name, they will not hesitate to report. And in most cases they don't stop until that fake profile is closed. A good con man doesn't want someone fighting to undermine their con. He is particularly careful to avoid them, as he goes for platforms that will not expose him. It will be painful to spend his time and energy trying to con his victim for months only for him to be exposed before getting paid. Prevention they say is better than cure and that rule is applicable in the con world too.

When they have carefully selected which platform to use, they need to make their profile look very real. As such they study the place and country they choose to pretend to be at. They also know the profession they claim to practice. They don't just come up with ambiguous details that they cannot live up to. They completely put their soul in it. Since they are looking for love, they always align their profile to reflect that. The con man could always indicate on his profile that he is single or divorced.

He is never in a rush in adding or accepting friends. He doesn't go about wasting his time on married women or teenagers. They are not what he needs in the scheme to be successful. The people he focuses his attention on are widows and single ladies. Mature ladies that are up to the age of tying the knot. He looks for widows or divorced single mothers. They are exactly in the category of being potential victims. The con man doesn't over add or request to be friends with this category of people at once to avoid being blocked by the social media platform as part of security measures employed by the site to prevent spamming.

He looks out for the fat and ugly ladies. The old ladies too who are lonely, retired and staying alone, category of people who will not have men making advances on them. Such people are secretly craving for attention and love. When the con man provides them with that, they will cross the red sea to please and do whatever he wants. So he is completely in for such people and the whole process is usually easy for him. He does everything to cut attention by posting good and enticing things. As ladies they are, they will not likely approach him first. So he understands he really has a lot of work to do by making them notice him.

He needs to often comment on their posts, always gracious and generous with his compliments. Finding a way to always align himself with his potential victims' opinion, but never too direct as to create the impression he was solely seeking their attention. With time, he tries and slide into their private message with "Hi "or "Hello". If they respond to him, he doesn't make the conversation about himself. He will do everything necessary to draw them out from their shell. Allowing them bare their hearts out as such people are most likely looking for someone to talk to. So the scammer tries to be that very person by being attentive to them.

The fraudster can't talk or discuss everything in one day. He must be patient to allow the concept of time to work its natural beauty. Occasionally, trying to find out how they were doing. They are women and prone to pride, he needs to be the one to start the chat. With time if they start liking him, then they will start participating actively. At this time he seeks for ways to communicate to them outside the platform he met them. Anyone who really likes him will want him to be in their life by giving him other ways of reaching out to her. It could be a phone number, email or anther social media platform.

Whichever one it is, he has to be the first to ask for it as an insurance policy. Just in case his fake profile gets blocked, which most times was likely going to happen. To the victim, the con man is just a caring man who wants other means to reach her always. The scammer must have created an email address to match their fake name. If she gives him an email address, she is probably going to be looking at such little detail to see if his story checks out. A good con man will not ignore that because such thing will make his mark suspicious of him. He would mail her regularly with romantic messages that she can't get elsewhere. If he is a good writer, he would compose such messages by himself. If not there are so many free sites that will give him access to such messages.

If his victims give him their mobile phone number which is most likely, he needs to have gotten a local phone number in the country he claims to be in. Some free or paid Apps will give him this in less than ten minutes. He would text her more often with romantic words. Since the scammer is not from where he says he is from, chances are that his accent is definitely different. The con man will try everything possible to avoid calls. If she insists and he has no option, then he tries to imitate the accent. In most cases, she will find out. The con man will quickly claim to have dual citizenship with a country that has entirely different accent and language. If she wants a video call, they are still Apps that will help him do that. He could also use two smart phones in faking a video call.

This actually requires high level of mastery. The procedure is complicated but can be learnt through practice. But he must always avoid audio calls and video calls. The con man concentrates more on chats and mailing. He keeps showering the victim with love and care by staying online always. He makes sure he is available to respond to them when they ever choose to. With time, the con man will come up with story that will require their victim's financial assistance or support. He creates a really good and touching story that will be very difficult for the victim to say no to. If they love him and have fallen for his lies, they will succumb to it.

As the case of every con man, he would start with small amount and with time, increases the amount. He creates a story that will put him in the position of being in constant need of financial help. It could be a reoccurring sickness or a fatal accident that requires multiple surgeries. He could claim to have a failing business which required funds to resuscitate. If they gave him the small amount he asked, they will give him any amount in subsequent times provided they have fallen in love with him. They can even sell or mortgage their property to provide him with that financial assistance.

Exposing internet fraudsters

CHAPTER FIVE

CRYPTO CURRENCY

Crypto currency is the new wave of money and financial game in the world. It is said to be the most and secured means of transactions. Its peculiarity lies in the anonymity of its users, very easy to use and prone to abuse as well. It has become the hub of cyber crimes.

One can easily collect ransom from a person or persons without being caught. Its payment route makes it completely undetectable and untraceable. Despite its negative tendencies, people still trust in it more than conventional means of transactions. The high security it operates by is something very commendable. Most platforms providing these crypto currencies have seven layered security measures. It's practically impossible to bypass. That's what most people think. Contrary to that, some scammers have a very high complicated way of bypassing the highly reverend security measures. All they do is take advantage of the loop holes in the system to perpetuate their heinous acts.

Stage one

This is actually the basis of all internet scam. These fraudsters are probably not yet ready to be an online con artist if they skip this stage. This is where they register and sign up for an email address. This will actually enable them access platforms on the web where they will be applying their trade.

Stage two

This is where they create fake profiles on social media platforms to apply their trade. In doing so, they need to impersonate someone who is good looking.

Stage three

This is where they go about on such online platforms in search for victims. They really spend so much time at this stage to find unsuspecting innocent people on the web. Those that will easily fall for their con

Stage four

This is where they play nice and cool. At this stage they really act saintly and brotherly to their friends on such online platforms. Such people are going to be made to believe in the fake life portrayed by these thieves.

Stage five

This is the final stage and the conclusion of every con, billing. This is where they show their true colors by coming up with ways for you to part with your hard earned income. If you are not careful you will lose your life savings to their scheming.

HOW THEY DO IT

This type of internet scam is relatively new and very rare. It is even unimaginable to convince someone that he or she can be scammed through crypto currency. The amount of trust and confidence people have in the security measures put in place by these virtual coin providers is very high. This is exactly what makes it easier for scammers to successfully apply their shameful trade. The suspicion is less or entirely absent. The con man capitalizes on that.

First thing as every con man doing online scam is that they get familiar with the little things. These are primary or fundamental things they put in place before starting the whole journey of scamming unsuspecting victims. They need to have a great knowledge on how to open an email address. It's not just signing up for email account but getting it done in a way that will have no traces back to them.

While doing so, they usually come up with a name that is entirely different from their real name. This is criminal activity; they don't and can't use their details in anything that has to do with it. They are very careful to avoid some of these silly mistakes that will inadvertently lead to them being caught.

When they are through with the creation of email, the next thing is to really think deep in the best place to find willing victims. They can always spend an ample time on the internet surfing and making researches on places to find who to con. It could be usual social media platforms or online dating sites. If they have money to pay for premium package in online dating site, it's usually the best. The reason being that most people on that platform are to some extent not broke.

They are looking for people they can scam of their money and looking for those that they feel have money is the wise thing to do. Some other free sites can still be valuable to them but most times a lot of broke people are all over the place since it's an all comer's affairs. Either free or premium sites, they can always find potential marks. Some people are not just good at spending on a website to chat and meet with strangers. That's not to say that they have no money. Whichever one the scammers choose, they are most definitely going to succeed. It all boils down to their determination and level of adroit maneuver. How good they are in deceiving and conning people. They must be able to sell the lies and persuade people to buy them even with their last dime.

When they have carefully chosen the platform, they need to find someone who they will impersonate. All they need is their pictures and videos. The scammer doesn't use his names. They craft out names that will suit the person's race and color. Such names correspond with the name they used in signing up for their fake email address. If it doesn't, they will create another email address to match whatever name they will be using to create a profile on any of the online platforms.

You might be wondering why it's important. It is very vital for these scammers to do so, to ensure that their story corresponds. Since the victims don't know the con man physically, he wouldn't want them to have any iota of doubts in their genuineness. There might come a time when the victim might need to send the scammer email. At such times, the email should have the same name as their fake profile. The con man is really crafty from the beginning and does the needful before the need arises. He is usually twenty steps ahead of his victims, putting his house in order, to prevent mumbling at any question that might come up at the course of his dealings with them.

It's very crucial the scammers know the kind of person they will be impersonating. Since its crypto currency they want to scam people on, they must be good and rich looking. They don't go copying some pictures of a broke man or lady. Nobody will believe them if they don't look rich and post pictures of rich experience. It is just the social media effect. People are easily carried away by the kind of lifestyle one fakes. He needs to look for someone that fits into that very category, someone that is constantly posting things about themselves, those drunk in their material possessions and enslaved in such obsession.

They must have pictures of them in their mansions. The con man needs videos of them doing some expensive adventures, pictures of them in their super expensive cars. The scammers really take their time to scout for such people, surfing through the internet on various websites for them. The person must be posting pictures regularly for the con man to always copy and use in their fake profile. He follows him with an account other than the fake one he wants to use in impersonating them. This is to give him access to their daily posts.

The scammers use such pictures to create his fake profile on any social media platform. It could be on the same website or entirely different one. Whichever one they choose, the person being impersonated will hardly find out since they are going to make use of a different name. They are hundreds of million people on such platforms and it is rare for them to spot fake profile. And these sites don't care if users have multiple accounts with varying names and pictures. The con man is just careful to avoid popular people that have crowds following them on social media.

When uploading on their fake profile, they start with the oldest picture/video. From oldest to new and to the newest as time passes by. They follow that procession; unsuspecting victims will believe that they are real. Since the person is bound to look younger in his or her old posts, they don't want people noticing some fishy things about the fake profile. The essence of fake account is for it to appear more original than the real one. When the scammer is too good in this, nobody will suspect a thing. Also, they have to be very patient. They don't go about posting plenty pictures at once to avoid running out of pictures. They complement the pictures and videos with write-ups suggestive of their expensive rich lifestyle.

When adding friends or following people on the social media platform they have chosen, they don't rush it. Being patient in doing so because too much of that will send a security risk threat to the site monitoring team. They might suspend the scammer's fake account or entirely block it. Some platforms don't put such restrictions or are just liberal with the number of people users follow. The scammers know exactly how each site works to be able to survive there. Since they are there for crypto currency scam, they need to have a wide range of different categories of people on their friend list. There is no limitation to who and who not to con in this type of scam, ranging from teens, to the oldest men and women. All they have to do is to be careful in doing so.

The scammer is so smart to allow some victims to add him. The victims are bound to do so once the scammer is active on such site. Most of the sites are programmed to suggest active users to other members for them to connect with each other. With the con man's rich lifestyle people will rush to become friends with him on that platform. When they add him, he doesn't accept all. He is very selective at this point, so as to send the good signal to the site management team. The idea of scam is simply appearing to be real and genuine. He doesn't want people suspecting the reason why he is on that platform.

The scammer really tries to maintain that mature and active presence in that site/platform. He will always post things that will suggest that he is the richest on his friends list. Constantly making people wish they were in his shoes. He is the embodiment of that perfect, smart and successful business man. It's always a winning day for him in the whole 365 days of the year. He intimidates all by making them look poor and unsuccessful. He doesn't bother trying to get closer to anyone for them to feel he wants love affair with them. Trying to be in love with anyone makes the con man look weak; he must embody that strength that comes with financial fulfillment and success.

If they must get close to anyone, it must be on a casual level. In most cases, the scammer could also pretend to be in search for that soul mate. It gets him the victim's trust quicker. But since most of them are not in that category he would concentrate more on talking business and investment with them, flooding them with his fake success. He appears to be generous to them. If he can afford to tip them with as little as $50 routinely he does so. The con artist will create more fake profiles and use them to praise himself. Such profiles comment and post lies of what he did for them.

He can even get someone real to make a video of them praising and thanking him for giving them huge sum of money in crypto currency. The person making the video is usually promised he or she will be gifted with large sums of money after making the video. With such promise the person makes it look as if the con man has already given them the money.

He or she showers the scammer with lots of compliments and extensively praising his generosity. You will be amazed how many people will be willing to do such video once such never-to-be -fulfilled promise is made to them. They are so many people who are online seeking for undue kindness from total strangers. The con man's rich and wealthy looking fake profile will make them worship him. They want a taste of his money without realizing that they will end up losing the little they have in the process. To them, the scammer is just a god-sent on a mission to help them. With this video, a lot of people will be eager to fall for the con.

The con man tells those that have bought the lies that he will assist them to set up a crypto currency wallet address. He convinces them that it will enable him send them the digital coin. When they finally set up the wallet address, he lies to them of sending the coin as earlier promised. The victim will check their wallet address and see nothing. Then they will contact him with complaints of not seeing anything. Then at this time the scammer will ask them to give him their login details to check the wallet address himself. Some people will hesitate, but he allays their fear by telling them they have nothing to fear since he was too rich to steal from them.

He convinces them that he is going to check the settings of the wallet address account to see why the coin he sent has not reflected. At this point the victim will agree because most of them are likely novice in crypto currency. Block chain is designed in such a way to send the user an email of confirmation in each time they try to login. This confirmation email comes with the details of where the attempt of login is made from. The scammer is smart to use V.P.N or R.D.P in logging in to correspond with the location he is pretending to be at. When he has successfully logged in, he gives it to a highly skilled hacker to send a fake coin.

This is very possible as the hacker takes the advantage of the system to manipulate the balance. They will manipulate the virtual coins that it will only reflect on the balance; when the owner wants to withdraw it will say insufficient funds. Then they will come back to him to complain again. At this time, he will tell the unsuspecting victims to buy a certain amount of coin to activate the wallet address so as to allow them access the huge coin he sent to them. The con man cooks up some story of how he sent the coin directly from a crypto currency mining company.

This he will tell them was the cause of them not being able to send the coin out. Since they have bought his lies of being rich and generous they are bound to accept this lie too. He is very smart to load their wallet address with huge coin to entice them. He could load like $100k dollars and ask them to put 10 % of that to access the money. Since human beings are constantly seeking for undue advantage, they will do as he says. Once they send the ten percent, with their login details which they gave him before, he will move the coin to his own real wallet address. Before they know what's happening he has taken their $10k worth of digital con.

This kind of scam looks so real. The fake loaded coin will be fluctuating also with the market price. No one will ever suspect it's fake. The con man studies everything about crypto currency to make it look real. This will enable him answer the litany of questions that will be directed at him from his potential victims. Since he will be claiming to send the huge sum of money in coin, he really needs to make his own fake wallet balance to run into millions. It's all necessary in selling the lies.

CHAPTER SIX

DECEASED

This is the kind of online scam that capitalizes on the possibility of people dying with their immediate family members not knowing where their wealth is stalked. It could be a secret safe hidden somewhere where the only person privy to its existence is the deceased. It could as well be a foreign based bank account with the deceased dying without leaving any clue behind on how to get the money. These things happen always and the underground criminal elements are now preying on this to defraud people with the promise of transferring to them whatever treasure the dead left behind.

Stage One

The scammer really needs to conjure up some enticing story. A false story of how some person died and left some treasures or money behind in some place. A location where only him was privy to and was determined to return it to someone who had the same surname as the deceased.

Stage two

At this very stage the con man really needs to go in hunt for email addresses or phone numbers. It is with these email addresses and phone numbers that they use in contacting potential victims.

Stage three

When any of them responds to their email by indicating interest, they will usually provide more details like fake documents, convincing the victim of the genuineness of their story.

Stage four

This stage is where the scammers tell the victim to forward their details to help process the repatriation of such treasure or money.

Stage five

This is where the scammer brings up reasons and need for the victims to pay a certain amount to facilitate the repatriation of the money.

HOW THEY DO IT

This very kind of scam is very popular and has been used by so many scammers in the past. The whole thing is centered on the con man been able to manipulate the greedy nature of so many people, the inordinate urge to reap where they never sowed. It is easy and simple if the scammer can assemble the right tools with a complementary good story to deceive their victims. First, they need to create an email address as it is the basis of online communications.

They need to sign up with a name that will correspond with maybe the bank or treasure holding company they intend to impersonate. If they can afford to buy a special domain name for that, they do so. This will really bring some genuineness to the whole scam. Since most likely the real domain name is taken, all they do is to buy something that is very similar to it. The difference could just be an alphabet or number. Not very many people will be so careful in reading every domain name letter by letter. They could also change the dot com to maybe dot org.

But some big companies are so popular and are highly protected from copycatting. This is due to their being highly prone to attackers. All the scammer does in this instance is misspelling it. If he cannot afford to buy the domain, then he goes for the free one, so many of them are out there online. All they need to do is to register it with similar name as the real official email address of the bank/company while using the free email address platform. People are so trusting or naive that they forget that most companies use paid domain. No serious company uses free email accounts to communicate with its customer's both old and prospective. Like I said before, not many people are aware of this simple rule and such people are bound to fall into this trap.

The scammers really need a large chunk of email addresses belonging to people. So they really come up with ways of extracting emails. They could use free email extractor. All they do is Google the keyword of people they intend to get their email address, copy the result page and paste all on the extractor then hit the extract button. It will bring out all the emails on the pages and sites selected. They could as well go through some sites where people openly display their email addresses and copy them. They are some PDF files of research works done by people which contain most times email address of a certain group of people. It could be farmers in a region or country.

All these methods are really tedious but very handy in giving the scammers what they want at no cost. If they decide they don't want to go through the stress, they go for paid extractor. A $200 worth of email extractor will give them access to millions of emails around the globe. All they do is to key in their search word. Automatically it will search thousands of sites for related articles. Some can give them as much as 50 thousand emails per hour. There is also an option to select all and copy them to their notepad which makes it really easy for them to set up a mailing list. From there they will run the email on another application that filters the bad or invalid emails. It will highlight the possible bad ones that will bounce back when they send the bulk message.

The scammers will also need to get an SMTP or mailer to assist them in sending the multiple emails. They go for paid platforms to send this large volume of emails. All the free email address platforms have limited number of emails one can send in a day. They don't have the luxury of having to wait each day to send a few emails to a few people. It really places restrictions and hampers on their progress. And also it is tedious to send as much as five hundred thousand emails. Imagine sending thirty emails per message. So it's usually best they make use of the premium mailing services. It simplifies the whole process by aiding them in the quantity of emails they send per minute. It also adds credibility and personifies it with the option of adding the name of the owner of the email in the message. It will make it look as though they were really sending them direct message.

When they are done with the problem of how to send bulk message at once, the next thing is for them, to really come up with a good story. It could be story of how a rich man that has the same name with their potential victim left some really huge amount of money in a secured vault. They usually claim that this vault is located in a country which is going to be different from that of their victim. That's why they need to know good information about their victims.

On the email, they will start by politely introducing themselves by choosing any name that will suit them and also claiming to be a lawyer representing a particular law firm in charge of whatever the client left behind. The victims are probably going to be wondering how the con man got their contact information as to be able to send them mail. So they lie to them they got it from the public records. Also, he tells them he was searching for a similar last name to that of his dead client who died through one natural disaster or another horrific tragedy.

This alone will arouse empathy and sympathy on the path of the victim. He goes on to tell them he was contacting them based on trust and confidentiality which will be necessary for the successful completion of the transaction. Before they go further they will apologize to the victims for the unsolicited mail. Telling them how they were aware that such means of contact was not the best approach to create a relationship of trust, but due to the circumstances at hand and the urgency of the claim that they were left with no option.

He goes ahead to tell the victims he was reaching them via email because of the immanent dangers of the vault where the treasure is stored being confiscated by the authorities. To entice them, the scammer needs to lie that the consignment is worth millions of dollars. That it was stored in a safe or a company domiciled in the country they were writing them from. Telling them the deceased never made disclosure of the exact content of the box and it was in a diplomatic box. That he kept it secret due to some security and personal reasons. As his attorney, he was supposed to find his family members to claim the treasure from the safe/holding company. The fraudster comes up with the story that the box will be confiscated, if he failed in his job to provide someone to inherit such property by the expiration of the ultimatum given to him by the company. They really sound concerned and bring this sense of duty to their tenses. This subsequently makes the victim feel this pity to assist, the obligation to do the right thing by ensuring that the deceased family got what belonged to them.

He really does everything necessary to convince the victim he has tried and made frantic efforts in search for a direct family member which was to no avail, he then decided to contact the victim. They will be suggesting to their victim to present their self as the beneficiary to this vault. He tells them he knew they may not be anyway related to his late client but having a common surname with him is a possibility that the content of the vault will be released to them.

The fraudster assures them that if they are willing and interested he will put in place all necessary modality in accordance with the law to legally present them as the true Next of Kin and true beneficiary. The scammer will extensively convince them that the transaction is 100% risk free as he has worked out all modalities to complete the operation effectively. Once the wealth is released to them, both of them shall divide the content in the ratio of 60% for them, and 40% for the scammer. They should write him back by indicating their interest to this letter either through any of the email they provide or they can call or send him a fax for further clarification. He persuades them to be quick in getting back to him, to affirm or reject the offer so as to enable him search for another person that bears similar last name.

The con thief could also work on the lie on how he was an attorney to some foreigner who died some years back with the family in a ghastly motor accident. He comes with the fake story, that his rich client who died and left behind assets in his country worth tens of millions of dollars.

In the mail, they could start by telling the victim it is a personal email that was specifically directed to them. As such they were hoping it will be treated as such. Explaining to them in details on how he was a solicitor to some rich guy who died with his immediate family members in a car accident. He goes on to tell the victims he has over the years since the client's death written to the embassy with the intent of finding a relative.

Such relative he hoped will claim the abandoned estates but his efforts have proved abortive. He became worried after he received an official letter from the authority of the bank where the money was deposited of their plans to confiscate the money in line with the law of the land. But he was lucky that the board of directors were magnanimous to grant him 14 working days to find his dead client's next of kin. If he failed they will have no option but confiscate the money. He will quote some laws to make his lies look more real. The victim is probably not going to be abreast with such laws since they were not in the same country.

He cooks up story of how he has investigated and discovered the plans of some members of the board of directors to divert the funds into their private account. Thus they were entirely on their selfish interest. When he confronted them with their evil plans they threatened to put the account in dormant status. If they did it will lead to relinquishing the money to the government which was clearly going to hurt him for failing his dead client.

By virtue of his closeness to the deceased and his immediate family, he was very much aware of his client's financial standing. He was sincerely pained by the death of his client, but had thought it will be unprofitable for his funds to be submitted to the government. Instead he has come up with a plan which was very professional. This plan entails legally presenting the victim as the next of kin of his deceased client which is legally possible and would be done in line with the law of the land. On this note he has decided to search for a credible person and finding that the victim bear a similar last name, he was compelled to contact them.

With their consent, he would present them to the bank as his late client's surviving family member so as to enable them put up a claim to the bank in that capacity as the next of kin to his client. The con man will usually tell the victim that the money was running into millions of dollars. This money will be easily paid to them before the account is declared dormant. He convinces them how legit his plans were and 100% risk free since he was in possession of every vital documents that would be required to confer their victim the legal right to make this claim. He tells them it was possible by the fact they bear a similar last name with his client, making it a lot easier for them to put up a claim in that capacity.

Therefore, to facilitate the immediate repatriation of this fund, they need to contact him via email address signifying their interest and as soon as he was confident of their trustworthiness, he will immediately intimate them with the complete details. The scammer will send to the victim documents, with which they will need to start up the whole process. He would also tell them of his readiness to direct them on how best to submit the application to the said bank.

If after some days the victim refused to respond and he was convinced the person would make a good mark, he would send them another mail. In that mail, he would emphasize to the victim the need to assist him. He tries to make the victim believe that they were the only person who has the same last name with his client he knew. Letting them know he was completely hoping and trusting in them to pull off this plan. He goes on telling them sweet things about his clients, how he was a philanthropist who would want his money to go into charity rather than the government seizing it.

The scammer could also come up with story of how his dead father left some large quantity of precious stones. Such stones he was willing to sell at a much reduced price. He could start by introducing himself to his victim as the eldest son of a king in one kingdom. A place that was renowned for its large deposit of natural precious stones.

He tells his victim how his father passed away leaving behind these stones for him and his siblings. Because of its value, everyone in the family was trying to outsmart the others by taking all of them. By virtue of him being the first son, his father was able to tell him the secret location of these stones before his demise. The con man will tell his victims that he has successfully moved these stones into a secured location which he was the only person on earth who knew the location. He is contacting them for the possibility of striking a business deal with them.

He would give more details of the stones and its current market value. For the scammer to know all these information, he would usually do his homework by finding out. Telling them he was willing to sell far below the market price because he was more interested in making sure he sold them before his siblings laid hands on them.

In all the instances given, the con man is always able to produce fake documents to back up his claims. In the event where an official domain email address is required, he would create one. He buys a local line of the country to further convince his victims. If he needs extra hands to collaborate his stories, he will come up with a ghost person by creating an email address which he too will be its handler in the guise it was another person. In the event it required phone calls and he cannot make the phone calls due to disparity in voice or accent, he will bring in a suitable co-conspirator. He doesn't leave anything to chance because the smallest suspicion can make his victims to grow cold feet. These criminals are very smart to put the necessary machinery in the perfect place.

CHAPER SEVEN

Lottery

Is the type of online scam that has to do with people being contacted for emerging as winners in a lottery. The contact comes through text message, call or mail. Most cases, the supposed winner never participated in the so called lottery. But the criminals usually come up with some stories to convince their victims they actually won. This type of scam has been around for a long time and people keep getting scammed on daily basis through it.

Stage one

They will contact you in any means they choose to. Most popularly is text message and email. They will write convincingly to make you believe that you won in some Promo.

Stage two

At this point they will ask you to contact them as an expression of your interest in claiming your winning.

Stage three

This stage is where they request for your contact information. These details they will tell you is to assist them in processing your winnings

Stage four

This is where they inform you that your winning has been successfully processed and was sent to you in any means they choose to.

Stage five

This is the final stage, the point where the scammer has been waiting for. It is his favorite stage. This is when they come up with some cock and bull stories on some hindrances making it difficult for them to deliver your winnings to you. They will also come up with the idea that you should pay some money to mitigate such challenges.

HOW THEY DO IT

For the scammer to be successful in this act, he needs to do an extensive homework. He needs to research on the kind of product he wants to fake their promo or lottery on. He prefers to take his time to actually ascertain whether such company has ever done a promo. If they have not, are they planning to do so in the nearest future? If so, it becomes necessary for him to take advantage of the public's anxious expectations.

He could just move his fake promo ahead of the real one. Most companies will not really give specific date and time they wish to run theirs. All they do most times is to give a hint on the period but no specifics. So, he uses that to his advantage as a con thief. If peradventure, the company has been running such promos in the past, it's also to his gain. All he needs to do is squeeze in his own fake promo in between the date and period of time the company does theirs. It will be difficult for the public to detect which one is real and fake. But he doesn't forget to be thorough in his findings. He is never in haste about the whole thing.

When he has found the possibility of the company doing the promo in the future or has done it in the past, he also needs to know about the company. Spending his quality time to find out about every little detail about the company, such details may include its registered name, founded date, its location or locations and the kind of services they render among other things. All these information will better guide him on how best to go about the whole scam process.

When he is contacting his victims, he would talk or write as someone that was informed. No one will listen to him if he starts telling them wrong things about the said company. The first thing people do is to Google about the company when they receive the scammer's promo message. If they find any discrepancies, they will ignore him and move on without responding to his message. As a con artist he doesn't want his scheming to end before it actually begins. He works consciously and assiduously to prevent this by staying alive to his responsibility of finding right information about the company.

The next thing is to find out if the company runs promos. If they do, how is it that they do it? Which set of people do they run the promo for. What's their message like? He finds out the range of amount they give to their winners. If not cash, what item do the winners win? How are these gifts or money transferred to these lucky winners? Is their promo always restricted to a certain location and place? He really needs to spend time to find all these and work on it. Because with the right information, it will be easier to even scam those that have won the real promo in the past.

If the company hasn't done the promo before, it's left for him to craft out his promo. He tries to get into the mind and thought of the company. He juxtaposes what exactly they would have done if they wanted to run a promotion. It is not a simple task, so he needs to have all the right information on the products and services they offer their target customers with regards to age and gender. And he would know their financial background so as to enable him come up with a realistic amount to be won in his fake promotion. He doesn't go promising to pay millions to lucky winners in a company that is financially struggling.

The idea of scam is to sell a lie and the best way to achieve that is present the victim lies that have factual backings. When they see that his information is accurate, they will easily buy into his lies and even convince others to do so. So the con thief is very meticulous in his findings. When he has done that perfectly well, he fears nothing because he is confident to see many gullible people who would fall for his scam. He will also find a target audience. The locality matters a whole lot.

A good scammer cannot start texting or mailing Americans resident in the USA that they won in promo of a company product that is not in the US. He needs to know the scope of the company's market. He bases his audience within that area. Anything outside that will not bring any desired outcome. Another challenge he will face is getting means of contacting them. Let's assume he chose text message. He would need to first buy an App that will help him send as many texts as possible in the shortest period of time. This scam is like fishing. He can't throw a narrow and small net and expect to catch fish. He needs to go with a big net and cast it in a large area of water body.

His chances at success are higher when his target area is wide. So buying such App will guarantee his success. Its price is very infinitesimal compared to what he stands to gain in the end. With such App he needs ways of getting multiple phone numbers of people. People he thinks fall within the category of those that will be users of the products. Some paid email extractor comes with phone number extractor. With such software, he is sure of laying hands on tens of thousands of local phone numbers of any country of his choice. If he doesn't want to use this software, he can sign up to premium sites, websites that provide the public with records of people. All he needs to do is to pay for a certain period of time and he will be provided with accurate phone numbers for him to do his bulk texting. If on the other hand he chose to make use of email in sending his fake promotion offer, he would need to get the necessary tools. Just like in the SMS case, he needs multiple valid emails to reach out to a larger number of people. Premium email extractor will be very useful in this regard. For him to dispatch the messages quicker and at a large scale, he also needs an enhanced tool. SMTP or mailer will just provide him with the best platform to do so.

He would also come up with a fake email account that resembles the company's. He can use free email address or paid domain to create a fake email address that will be hard to detect. With the mailer, he can always input which ever email address he wants the receiver to see as the sender. He would also need the local phone number of the country where the company is located. If they will be need for any phone calls, hiring a female conspirator is always best. In the case he cannot find any, he twists his raspy and harsh male voice to sound more polite on the phone.

He could also carry out this kind of scam on social media platforms. To do that he really needs to create a good profile that looks very official on such site. Post things on his timeline that will suggest that he is an official in that very site. His posts will be things that will be related to promoting the good image of the site.

He does it for months and starts adding and following friends. Then after awhile he starts contacting people directly on their private message on the social media platform.

He can start by telling the victim of how he was inquiring whether they have been informed of their winning and if they even knew the platform was doing a promo. They are bound to say no because of a truth there was no such promo. The victims are likely going to tell him to proceed with his information. Then he would congratulate them of their winnings of a huge amount of money being offered by the site to selected lucky winners. He tries to convince them it was legit and they have nothing to be afraid of. He can give them a spam link he has created that looks official, to collaborate his story.

They are most likely going to click on the link. When they do, they will believe him the more as the page will look very genuine. Once the victim indicates interest in claiming his winning, the scammer will then ask them to pay a token to enable the platform process their winnings. With their mind set on the big prize he told them they had won, they will comply almost immediately. He could claim that the fee was for a courier service to deliver the prize.

He can also use fake social media platform, something like Grant Processing Agent and Global Financial Facility. In this type of scam the con thief needs to hack the account of users and spam their friend lists.

They will not suspect a thing since the message will be coming from their trusted friend on that platform. They will never find out their friend's account was hacked, since they probably have no other means of reaching out among themselves. He starts by telling them how he saw their name on the winners' list of some global financial organization. He convinces them to contact this so called organization. In order to wet their financial appetite and make them act quickly the scammer quotes a really big amount of money as what they won. The money would run into hundreds of thousands in dollars. When they contact the said organization, a fake agent will be assigned to them. Who will in the end tell the victim to pay some amount of money to help process their winning. The money is usually at a very low percentage when compared to the star prize.

He could also take this scam to a whole new level by involving millions of people. In this kind, the scammer will mail the person and congratulates him or her on their winning in some lottery that was conducted among thousands of companies and email address of millions of people around the world. Telling them of how they were being lucky to have won a certain amount of money running into millions. They were required to keep their winnings secret as to avoid unscrupulous people from claiming what belongs to them.

This very advice is to prevent the victim from telling someone that could be reasonable enough to suspect that this is a scam. The scammer is usually very careful to prevent his potential victims from discussing what he tells them with a third party. He encourages them to maintain secrecy during the transaction for their own good. To make it look real he tells them to come to a certain location in a far country. They will most likely not agree to come but they now trusted him.

Then he asks them to mail their personal details to a certain attorney to help them claim their winnings. The victims would be told to do so with the details of their winnings. Such details may include their ticket number or special code assigned to them. He would emphasize on the need for them to be fast about it, threatening them by telling them that the organization will invalidate any prize that remains unclaimed at the end of a short of time. This will bring this spirit of urgency in them. When they finally contact the said attorney to process their winnings, they will become more convinced of the genuineness of his fake promo. The scammer will not rush into asking for his victims to pay anything yet. He makes sure that the person is deeply submerged in his con. Then at that point he can ask for them to pay a certain amount of money as processing fee.

CHAPTER EIGHT

Fake parcel

This is more like online dating, because for the fraudster to send parcel to anyone there must have been something between the both parties. The scammers don't just send parcel to some random or strange person and expect them to cooperate with their fraudulent antics. So we shall basically go through all it will take to date and get someone's trust. We shall outline exactly what we have in chapter four where we talked about online dating.

This is the particular type of scam where the victim is tricked into paying some clearance fee in anticipation of getting a parcel that was sent to them. In this case, there was never any parcel to start with. It is based on idea of chasing the shadow.

First stage

They need to create an email address, which is more like the ABCD of every form of internet communications. With this, they can access and sign up on any social media platforms, dating sites inclusive. The scammer would also create a fake courier service site or find someone in the criminal world who owns one.

Second stage

This is the stage where they go in hunt for potential victims. In order to achieve this, these scammers need convincing profiles on these online platforms, with really good looking and enticing pictures. Videos too are regularly uploaded by these unscrupulous people.

Third stage

This is where they make contact by directly messaging their victims on these platforms; they really play nice and all caring. They try to get their victims to fall in love with them.

Fourth stage

This is the stage where the con thief sends a parcel to their victim. Unlike in online dating where the scammer has no intentions or does not know how to send fake parcel to their victim.

HOW THEY DO IT

This very form of scam requires so much from the scammer in terms of time because he is going to be in people's lives. He has to be online steady to always chat with his victims and respond to their messages. He becomes ultimately their source of joy; he must be available to live up to it. He is usually prepared. For a start, he needs to create an email account with the name, age and gender of who he chooses to impersonate. He could still pretend to be a man even if he was actually a woman or vice versa. But since women are rare in this line of work, mostly it is men pretending to be women.

Men can also pretend to be other men with corresponding name and race. They need to choose wisely on which one suits their capability. They have to create that email address to reflect all these things. They have to make sure the names tally with what they will use on the social media platforms. This is just in case if their victims want to write them through email. It's amateur for these scammers to give their email address that doesn't tally with their name. They are very careful at this stage because it's the foundation which will determine their success or failure. Using a password they could always remain is also vital. As trivia as it seem, it's really important to them.

The next stage is for them to move on to any social media platform. But just before they do so, they need pictures and videos of someone they will be impersonating. The person must really look good and attractive. It's dating, so they need to appear charming and sexy. All they need to do is to spend really good quality time on Facebook or Instagram to search for individuals who are constantly posting their pictures. With the help of some App they can download the pictures and videos seamlessly. These scammers avoid individuals that are popular like celebrities.

They cannot impersonate such people for long without running into their fans. The scheme will fail when they use such people even in the most secret and relatively unknown websites. The online thieves copy as much of the persons pictures and videos as possible. This is just to avoid running into trouble if the person blocks him from viewing their profile. To be on the safe side, they don't comment on such people's posts to avoid provoking them. They are just their silent friend or follower. With this, the scammer can always have access to copy their pictures at the least possible suspicion from such people.

Daily and regularly they have to make their fake profile look real by uploading those impersonating materials. They are careful not to over post such materials to avoid looking desperate. They don't have to post too many pictures at once. No one does that kind of thing. Such acts are not good in the crime world. The scammer has to complement the photos/videos with good posts of really crafted inspiring sentences. The fraudster posts about his daily activities, family and things happening around the world. They live and embody the life of that person they are impersonating.

They replicate exactly what the person could be doing on the daily by using their pictures to make these conjectures. If the scammer cannot imagine and come up with this idea, then they copy the lifestyle of that person if it suits their plan. But usually it doesn't, because the real person is living a true life and probably not interested in wooing people into online dating. On the other hand the scammer was solely on the online platform for making people fall in love with him. So, its best they come up with their own style while at the same time using the person's pictures and videos. They also refrain from using posts that contain specificity with locations.

The professional con men never use the same location as the person they are impersonating. It will be easier for people to catch them; it could be their friends, relations or them personally. And while posting their pictures, the con man is very observant to study the picture very well. The background can expose his lie. For instance; if he was claiming to be in London and in the picture of the person, there is a Las Vegas street number or symbol. With this, people can easily detect and find out he is lying. Even in the videos he will be posting, he is also really careful.

They don't post a video of someone they are impersonating carrying out a surgery as a surgeon while on their fake profile they claim to be an engineer. Or posting a picture with rivers/water in the background when their fake profile says they live in a desert-like region. All these little slip-ups will expose them instantly. Some people are fond of sniffing around, they will spot such discrepancies.

While taking into cognizance of these details, the scammer knows he is also required to be careful with the kind of people he adds as his friends on these social media platforms. There are many scammers who were also there with the same objective as him. He is there to scam others and can't scam his kind. It could be likened to a snake trying to swallow its kind. And these fake accounts of his kind will also put the scammer in trouble, especially if they are controlled by amateur con men.

The system will easily block and blacklist them when people complain about them, which most likely it's possible. When this happens and they form a greater percentage of his friend list, he is definitely going to taste their misery. It's like mingling with the unhappy. It was just a matter of time before you become sad and depressed like them too. A professional con man avoids such people as much as he can. It's easy to do so, since he already knows how a con man behaves. Once they reflect his fake and impersonating style, he cuts them off or never accepts them in the first place. To be on the safer side, he would usually go through their profile before requesting or accepting to be their friend on those social media platforms.

As he is screening to avoid his kind, he is also keen to select those that will easily fall for his scheming. Let's assume he was acting to be a lady, his focus would be on men, single or divorced. They are so many men on the internet, who are solely there to cheat on their wife. He could be lucky to find such people, they are usually easier to con. The scammer presents them with the fantasy they are desperately craving for. He spots such people through their profile. He checks if it says married, how often they post things about their marriage. Such men don't usually talk about their wife or kids. If he monitors them very well, he will notice their marital misery which is reflected on their social media lifestyle. The way such men comment on posts and their opinions on issues relating to marriage and family. As little and irrelevant it may sound, it's actually very important to his success or failure.

So he scrolls through their profiles before sending them friend request or following them. He doesn't have to waste his time on unproductive victims. Then for the single men, the scammer is very careful to select those that he feels could be ready or mostly interested in marriage. He avoids men who are always posting pictures of where they are in the company of beautiful women. Such men have real life sexual happiness and will be extremely difficult to have them fall for his trick. The con man targets the single men who are somewhat shy and look unhappy. Those who are always posting work related things.

Chances are they don't have love life and will be prone to fall into his trap easily. Another people in his radar are the widowers. Of cause not those that their spouse just died. Such people are difficult for the scammer to scam. They are most likely still moaning and will not have that time to start listening to him. But if he chooses to go after them, it could actually act in his favor. He plays and acts nice towards them, living in their misery with them. If possible he acts more touched and pained than the bereaved. He becomes their shoulder they will cry on and that person to lean on in their moaning moment. When they are completely healed and they don't have a lady in their life, they will fall for the scammer.

He also goes after older and fat looking men, men who are easily rejected by young girls in real life. Most of them are on the internet to try their luck. Chances are they have witnessed multiple and endless disappointments from women. Some of them too might just be sexual perverts with high libido. They are in desperate need of how and who to satisfy their animalistic urge with. From the scammer's fake sexy and good looking pictures and videos, they will easily believe her to be real because they are not thinking straight. The con man is quick to add and accept people like that.

He concentrates on adding many of them, they are his potential victims. While adding them he is smart not to over add them at once. Bit by bit, in order not to arouse security suspicion from the website. The online platform is most likely going to block his account if they noticed the unusual adding of people. So he is patient and takes it slow. He understands that the world belongs to the patient man. Most times he comments and likes their post instead of adding them. Some will be moved to add him because of his comments especially when he praises or aligns himself with their opinion. In so doing, they are creating that aura of genuineness for his fake profile. This will also trick the security measures put in place by the platform.

When he finally becomes friends or starts following them, he is never too quick to start conversations with them. Since he was pretending to be a lady, they will come for her. Men see themselves as hunters in the game of sexual adventures. So he leaves them to make the first contact. But he makes frantic efforts for them to notice him. He is continuously being on their face, posting good and enticing pictures and things. He responds to their comments with cheerfulness, adopting the customer care service or waitress approach. Being graceful in her words as a lady he pretends to be. Giving off the impression, she is up for grasp. Most of the people who are going to fall victim are mostly shy people.

They need that reassurance that they will succeed if they approached her. They could have likely failed multiple times in the past in their love life. So they need that good motivation to boast their confidence level. The scammer tries to give them all these without looking desperate of wanting a man. If they suspect this, chances are they will avoid him. Some will look at him as a scam he is. Others that would want a serious relationship with him will back trace their steps. Nobody really wants a desperate woman. She appears happy and comfortable as a single lady. From time to time he also comments on the post of those who regularly comment on his. He doesn't remain on the high horse of female ego and pride. He tries to reciprocate the love too

This will send the needed message. People are naturally drawn to those who are drawn to them. When the victims notice this, then they will waste no time in making the first contact, which the scammer is anxiously looking for. Before long, men will flood his inbox with messages. At this point he doesn't rush into accepting and giving off the impression he wants them so bad. Men value what cost them much to acquire. The con man understands not to be too quick and cheap to accept any of them. While playing on this card, he makes sure he is not too costly for them. No man wants to spend his entire time chasing after something that will cost him all he has got. Except those that are driven by the wild wind of blind love. They are just few and when they are shown little love and care by other ladies; they will opt in for them. In the end the con man becomes a loser. So he doesn't play too hard to get or too easy to get. He maintains a balance!

At first, some of them will be bold to tell him in clear terms what they need. He is not going to hastily accept their proposal. Softly, he turns them down while keeping them in the friend zone. In essence, he makes the whole affair less romantic in the beginning. He avoids not playing the card of a hooker. Unless he was acting as one, then he would accept and bill them immediately.

But since he was not, he needs to bring that aura and pride of womanhood in play. Creating the impression that he was not in a hurry, but he maintains the friendship. This will give him an ample time to study the person very well and know if they are real or not. This time also will be valuable to him as they will be more eager to please and woo her. If he finally decides to open up for any of them, he doesn't publicize it by posting about it. He was on that platform for business and he needs as many "customers" as possible. Being private about it and indirectly suggests to them to keep what was going between them a secret. If not, other potential victims will take off. They need to live in the illusion that she is not taken yet. This will give him the opportunity to trap as many victims as possible in his cobweb of scam.

When he finally gets into serious commitment with them, he allows them to always start up the conversation. Letting them be on the driving seat but he must subtly control how they steer the ship in the friendship. This is typical of ladies. The scammer knows he must act that way. They are usually going to ask for other ways to reach her other than the usual chats. If the online platform allows audio or video calling, they are bound to call him. Since he is a man posing as a woman he wouldn't answer the call to prevent his victims from finding out his true identity.

He comes up with some really good excuse why he can't answer such calls. He could tell them her place of work doesn't allow workers answering phone or video calls. Some will want to find out when she is usually at home so as to call her during such free time, because no one works round the clock. In this case, he tells them but he will not come online those periods of time. This will give the impression that she is always exhausted after work and rests at home. In conclusion she doesn't have time. This is a perfect excuse for awhile.

But if things really get intense and serious, the victims will need her phone number. He is not in the place or country he claims to be, so getting their local phone number becomes the issue. But it's just simple for the experts. There are so many Apps that offer such services. Some of them are entirely free or relatively cheap. With that he can have the local phone number of any country in the world.

All he needs is a good and strong internet connection to use such numbers. Since he is a man and wouldn't want his masculine voice spoil things for him, he gets them to text him instead of calling. In the event they insist on hearing her voice he has no option than to buy a voice changer. With this tool he can twist his voice to sound feminine. When doing so, he doesn't prolong the call. He keeps it short to avoid getting caught. Such tools are usually not 100% efficient as their manufacturers want you to believe. The con man understands the importance of playing safe. If he cannot get such tools, getting a real girl to make the call is the second best option.

It will make the whole thing look real. All he needs to do is to intimate the girl with what she will say and not say. If possible draft an essay, putting down word to word all she needs to say. While making such calls, he puts it on loud speaker to help monitor the call. He can easily control things by signaling her when to keep quiet and when to talk. She must really sound sexy for the sexually perverted men. Then she also sounds official and responsible for the responsible ones. In all, her voice must blend into the occasion.

If it calls for video calling and it becomes mandatory for him to do so, they are Apps that people don't know exist that will assist him. Most people know and use such Apps without knowing its full potency in the criminal world. With such Apps he can load the person's pre-recorded video and allow it to play. Then play it for few seconds and ends it. When the victims ask what happened, he is usually very quick to blame the internet connectivity.

Most times once they have seen such short video they are usually convinced that she is real. If it's a nude video, it will get the man's head popping.

However, if the scammer chose to impersonate a man, then he needs to be ready to act like a man in need of love. First, he searches on different platforms on the internet for a suitable person to impersonate. He is very careful in putting some small details into consideration. These details if neglected will spell his doom in the con venture. So he doesn't leave anything to chance. He has to consider the age, race and physical appearance. At what age would a man be and he will be easily attractive to women on the internet.

What race is easier to find women tripping for them? And the physique is also very vital too. He cannot look dull and be sexually appealing to women. He has to find that handsome man with good physique. It's not compulsory he must be athletic. An average healthy looking man will fit into what the scammer is looking for. As a professional he doesn't go impersonating someone popular. He makes sure he changes their name, location and all the details about them. All he wants is their pictures and videos.

When he has seen a good example of this, he will proceed to creating a profile on any social media platform or in an online dating site. Dating sites are usually easier and better. Their double ganger is most likely not on such dating platforms. If he is truly handsome, ladies in real life will flock around him so much that he will hardly have extra time to look for love on the internet. This will act in the con man's favor by making sure his cover doesn't get blown.

Because if the person were to see that someone was using his pictures on a different name, they will not hesitate to report. And in most cases they don't stop until that fake profile is closed. A good con man doesn't want someone fighting to undermine their con. He is particularly careful to avoid them, as he goes for platforms that will not expose him. It will be painful to spend his time and energy trying to con his victim for months only for him to be exposed before getting paid. Prevention they say is better than cure and that rule is applicable in the con world too.

When they have carefully selected which platform to use, they need to make their profile look very real. As such they study the place and country they choose to pretend to be at. They also know the profession they claim to practice. They don't just come up with ambiguous details that they cannot live up to. They completely put their soul in it. Since they are looking for love, they always align their profile to reflect that. The con man could always indicate on his profile that he is single or divorced.

He is never in a rush in adding or accepting friends. He doesn't go about wasting his time on married women or teenagers. They are not what he needs in the scheme to be successful. The people he focuses his attention on are widows and single ladies. Mature ladies that are up to the age of tying the knot. He looks for widows or divorced single mothers. They are exactly in the category of being potential victims. The con man doesn't over add or request to be friends with this category of people at once to avoid being blocked by the social media platform as part of security measures employed by the site to prevent spamming.

He looks out for the fat and ugly ladies. The old ladies too who are lonely, retired and staying alone, category of people who will not have men making advances on them. Such people are secretly craving for attention and love. When the con man provides them with that, they will cross the red sea to please and do whatever he wants. So he is completely in for such people and the whole process is usually easy for him. He does everything to cut attention by posting good and enticing things. As ladies they are, they will not likely approach him first. So he understands he really has a lot of work to do by making them notice him.

He needs to often comment on their posts, always gracious and generous with his compliments. Finding a way to always align himself with his potential victims' opinion, but never too direct as to create the impression he was solely seeking their attention. With time, he tries and slide into their private message with "Hi "or "Hello". If they respond to him, he doesn't make the conversation about himself. He will do everything necessary to draw them out from their shell. Allowing them bare their hearts out as such people are most likely looking for someone to talk to. So the scammer tries to be that very person by being attentive to them.

The fraudster can't talk or discuss everything in one day. He must be patient to allow the concept of time to work its natural beauty. Occasionally, trying to find out how they were doing. They are women and prone to pride, he needs to be the one to start the chat. With time if they start liking him, then they will start participating actively. At this time he seeks for ways to communicate to them outside the platform he met them. Anyone who really likes him will want him to be in their life by giving him other ways of reaching out to them. It could be a phone number, email or anther social media platform.

Whichever one it is, he has to be the first to ask for it as an insurance policy. Just in case his fake profile gets blocked, which most times was likely going to happen. To the victim, the con man is just a caring man who wants other means to reach her always. The scammer must have created an email address to match their fake name. If she gives him an email address, she is probably going to be looking at such minute details to see if his story checks out. A good con man will not ignore that because such things will make his mark suspicious of him. He would mail her regularly with romantic messages that she can't get elsewhere. If he is a good writer, he would compose such messages by himself. If not they are so many free sites that gives him access to such messages.

If his victims give him their mobile phone number which is most likely, he needs to have gotten a local phone number in the country he claims to be in. Some free or paid Apps will give him this in less than ten minutes. He would text her more often with romantic words. Since the scammer is not from where he says he is from, chances are that his accent is different. The con man will try everything possible to avoid calls. If she insists and he has no option, then he tries to imitate the accent. In most cases, she will find out. The con man will quickly claim to have dual citizenship with a country that has entirely different accent and language. If she wants a video call, they are still Apps that will help him do that. He could also use two smart phones in faking a video call.

This actually requires high level of mastery. The procedure is complicated but can be learnt through practice. But he must always avoid audio calls and video calls. The con man concentrates more on chats and mailing. He keeps showering the victim with love and care by staying online always. He makes sure he is available to respond to them when they ever choose to.

With time, he comes up with some story that will require he sends them all or some of his valuables. It could be that he was deeply connected to her that he wishes to give her some special gifts. The scammer could also tell the victim he was planning of settling down with them and it was necessary he sent his valuables to them. Or his valuables were at risk of being stolen from him due to the high level of insecurity in the country or region he is.

The summary of it all is just for the con man to get the trust of his victim. They need to fall in love with him or he makes them believe he loves them. The kind of love that will make him give them anything money could buy. Once they have bought this lie, the next thing he does is to send them a parcel containing jewelry and other expensive things. To make it look real he needs to build a courier website of his own.

The victims will not know it's fake because the scammer is good in masking the identity of the owner of the site during hosting. All he would do is get pictures of a box which the victim assumes is what he is sending to them. The site will generate a unique code to convince the victim that a parcel was sent through the site. The code is usually in form of tracking number. The con man will encourage them to login and check the location of their parcel regularly. They will not suspect any foul play if the courier site is properly designed and hosted.

He could also tell them that he has paid every necessary fee to ensure the parcel gets to them. The scammer usually discontinues or reduces every form of communication with the victim. The site after some days will contact the victim to inform her of the parcel being seized in some country border because it contained some large sums of cash. That she is required to pay for the clearing of the parcel if she doesn't want it permanently seized. The victim will get back to the scammer but he will tell her he was presently unable to access funds to send to them. He encourages them to pay that he would repay them once his ship decks. Since the amount is usually small compared to the worth of the valuables inside the parcel, the victims are usually compelled to pay by virtue of human greed.

After some days again the scammer will contact the victim through the fake courier site to come up with another story to make them pay money. He would keep doing this till the victim realizes it's all but scam. Sometimes it usually takes a long time for the victim to come to terms with that. They have trusted and loved him for a long period of time; it becomes difficult to start doubting him. Some will even keep borrowing to continue paying for the charges so as to ensure they get the parcel. To commit them very well, the con man would tell them the parcel contained some very vital documents he cannot afford to lose. This will make them do everything necessary to avoid the permanent seizure of the parcel at every given time the courier site tells them it was being temporarily held.

CHAPTER NINE

Fake bank account

This type of scam is where one tricks you into a bank page that looks like the real bank page. In this page the victim will see a big account balance in the fake account. Usually, they are tricked by someone they have been chatting and dating online. The victims most likely trust and believe the con man would not lie to them. They also would have told the lie that they are wealthy and rich enough to give the victim hundreds of thousands in dollars. This is also more like online dating because they contact their victims through the internet and make them fall in love with them.

First stage

They need to create an email address, which is more like the ABCD of every form internet communications. With this, the can access and sign up on any social media platforms, dating sites inclusive. They would also need a spam page of the bank the fraudster chooses to work with.

Second stage

This is the stage where they go in hunt for potential victims. In order to achieve this, these scammers need convincing profiles on these online platforms with really good looking and enticing pictures. Videos too are regularly uploaded by these unscrupulous people.

Third stage

This is where they make contact by directly messaging their victims on these platforms; they really play nice and all caring. They try to get you to fall in love with them.

Fourth stage

At this final stage is where the scammer presents the victim with an opportunity to assist him. These fraudsters make it enticing by making the account balance to really have big money in it.

HOW THEY DO IT

This very form of scam requires so much from the scammer in terms of time because he is going to be in people's lives. He has to be online steady to always chat with his victims and respond to their messages. He becomes ultimately their source of joy; he must be available to live up to it. He is usually prepared. For a start, he needs to create an email account with the name, age and gender of who he chooses to impersonate. He could still pretend to be a man even if he was actually a woman or vice versa. But since women are rare in this line of work, mostly it is men pretending to be women.

Men can also pretend to be other men with corresponding name and race. They need to choose wisely on which one suits their capability. They have to create that email address to reflect all these things. They have to make sure the names tally with what they will use on the social media platforms. This is just in case if their victims want to write them through email. It's amateur for these scammers to give their email address that doesn't tally with their name. They are very careful at this stage because it's the foundation which will determine their success or failure. Using a password they could always remember is also vital. As trivia as it seem, it's really important to them.

The next stage is for them to move on to any social media platform. But just before they do so, they need pictures and videos of someone they will be impersonating. The person must really look good and attractive. It's dating, so they need to appear charming and sexy. All they need to do is to spend really good quality time on Face book or Integra to search for individuals who are constantly posting their pictures. With the help of some App they can download the pictures and videos seamlessly. These scammers avoid individuals that are popular like celebrities.

They cannot impersonate such people for long without running into their fans. The scheme will fail when they use such people even in the most secret and relatively unknown websites. The online thieves copy as much of the persons pictures and videos as possible. This is just to avoid running into trouble if the person blocks him from viewing their profile. To be on the safe side, they don't comment on such people's posts to avoid provoking them. They are just their silent friend or follower. With this, the scammer can always have access to copy their pictures at the least possible suspicion from such people.

Daily and regularly they have to make their fake profile look real by uploading those impersonating materials. They are careful not to over post such materials to avoid looking desperate. They don't have to post too many pictures at once. No one does that kind of thing. Such acts are not good in the crime world. The scammer has to complement the photos/videos with good posts of really crafted inspiring sentences. The fraudster posts about his daily activities, family and things happening around the world. They live and embody the life of that person they are impersonating.

They replicate exactly what the person could be doing on the daily by using their pictures to make these conjectures. If the scammers cannot imagine and come up with this idea, then they copy the lifestyle of that person if it suits their plan. But usually it doesn't, because the real person is living a true life and probably not interested in wooing people into online dating. On the other hand the scammer was solely on the online platform for making people fall in love with him. So, its best they come up with their own style while at the same time using the person's pictures and videos. They also refrain from using posts that contain specificity with locations.

The professional con men never use the same location as the person they are impersonating. It will be easier for people to catch them; it could be their friends, relations or them personally. And while posting their pictures, the con man is very observant to study the picture very well. The background can expose his lie. For instance; if he was claiming to be in London and in the picture of the person, there is a Las Vegas street number or symbol. With this, people can easily detect and find out he is lying. Even in the videos he will be posting, he is also really careful.

They don't post a video of someone they are impersonating carrying out a surgery as a surgeon while on their fake profile they claim to be an engineer. Or posting a picture with rivers/water in the background when their fake profile says they live in a desert-like region. All these little slip-ups will expose them instantly. Some people are fond of sniffing around, they will spot such discrepancies.

While taking into cognizance of these details, the scammer knows he is also required to be careful with the kind of people he adds as his friends on these social media platforms. There are many people who were also there with the same objective as him. He is there to scam others and can't scam his kind. It could be likened to a snake trying to swallow its kind. And these fake accounts of his kind will also put the scammer in trouble, especially if they are controlled by amateur con men.

The system will easily block and blacklist them when people complain about them, which most likely it's possible. When this happens and they form a greater percentage of his friend list, he is definitely going to taste their misery. It's like mingling with the unhappy. It was just a matter of time before you become sad and depressed like them too. A professional con man avoids such people as much as he can. It's easy to do so, since he already knows how a con man behaves. Once they reflect his fake and impersonating style, he cuts them off or never accepts them in the first place. To be on the safer side, he would usually go through their profile before requesting or accepting to be their friend on those social media platforms.

As he is screening to avoid his kind, he is also keen to select those that will easily fall for his scheming. Let's assume he was acting to be a lady, his focus would be on men, single or divorced. So many men are on the internet to cheat on their wife. He could be lucky to find such people, they are usually easier to con. The scammer presents them with the fantasy they are desperately craving for. He spots such people through their profile. He checks if it says married, how often they post things about their marriage. Such men don't usually talk about their wife or kids. If he monitors them very well, he will notice their marital misery which is reflected on their social media lifestyle. The way such men comment on posts and their opinions on issues relating to marriage and family. As little and irrelevant it may sound, it's actually very important to his success or failure.

So he scrolls through their profiles before sending them friend request or following them. He doesn't have to waste his time on unproductive victims. Then for the single men, the scammer is very careful to select those that he feels could be ready or mostly interested in marriage. He avoids men who are always posting pictures of where they are in the company of beautiful women. Such men have real life sexual happiness and will be extremely difficult to have them fall for his trick. The con man targets the single men who are somewhat shy and look unhappy. Those who are always posting work related posts.

Chances are they don't have love life and will be prone to fall into his trap easily. Another people in his radar are the widowers. Of cause not those that their spouse just died. Such people are difficult for the scammer to scam. They are most likely still moaning and will not have that time to start listening to him. But if he chooses to go after them, it could actually act in his favor. He plays and acts nice towards them, living in their misery with them. If possible he acts more touched and pained than the bereaved. He becomes their shoulder they will cry on and that person to lean on in their moaning moment. When they are completely healed and they don't have a lady in their life, they will fall for the scammer.

He also goes after older and fat looking men, men who are easily rejected by young girls in real life. Most of them are on the internet to try their luck. Chances are they have witnessed multiple and endless disappointments from women. Some of them too might just be sexual perverts with high libido. They are in desperate need of how and who to satisfy their animalistic urge with. From the scammer's fake sexy and good looking pictures and videos, they will easily believe her to be real because they are not thinking straight. The con man is quick to add and accept people like that.

He concentrates on adding many of them, they are his potential victims. While adding them he is smart not to over add them at once. Bit by bit, in order not to arouse security suspicion from the website. The online platform is most likely going to block his account if they noticed the unusual adding of people. So he is patient and takes it slow. He understands that the world belongs to the patient man. Most times he comments and likes their post instead of adding them. Some will be moved to add him because of his comments especially when he praises or aligns himself with their opinion. In so doing, they are creating that aura of genuineness for his fake profile. This will also trick the security measures put in place by the platform.

When he finally becomes friends or starts following them, he is never too quick to start conversations with them. Since he was pretending to be a lady, they will come for her. Men see themselves as hunters in the game of sexual adventures. So he leaves them to make the first contact. But he makes frantic efforts for them to notice him. He is continuously being on their face, posting good and enticing pictures and things. He responds to their comments with cheerfulness, adopting the customer care service or waitress approach. Being graceful in her words as a lady he pretends to be. Giving off the impression, she is up for grasp. Most of the people who are going to fall victim are mostly shy people.

They need that reassurance that they will succeed if they approached her. They could have likely failed multiple times in the past in their love life. So they need that good motivation to boast their confidence level. The scammer tries to give them all these without looking desperate of wanting a man. If they suspect this, chances are they will avoid him. Some will look at him as a scam he is. Others that would want a serious relationship with him will back trace their steps. Nobody really wants a desperate woman. She appears happy and comfortable as a single lady. From time to time he also comments on the post of those who regularly comment on his. He doesn't remain on the high horse of female ego and pride. He tries to reciprocate the love too

This will send the needed message. People are naturally drawn to those who are drawn to them. When the victims notice this, then they will waste no time in making the first contact, which the scammer is anxiously looking for. Before long, men will flood his inbox with messages. At this point he doesn't rush into accepting and giving off the impression he wants them so bad. Men value what cost them much to acquire. The con man understands not to be too quick and cheap to accept any of them. While playing on this card, he makes sure he is not too costly for them. No man wants to spend his entire time chasing after something that will cost him all he has got. Except those that are driven by the wild wind of blind love. They are just few and when they are shown little love and care by other ladies; they will opt in for them. In the end the con man becomes a loser. So he doesn't play too hard to get or too easy to get. He maintains a balance!

At first some of them will be bold to tell him in clear terms what they need. He is not going to hastily accept their proposal. Softly, he turns them down while keeping them in the friend zone. In essence, he makes the whole affair less romantic in the beginning. He avoids playing the card of a hooker. Unless he was acting as one, then he would accept and bill them immediately.

But since he was not, he needs to bring that aura and pride of womanhood in play. Creating the impression that he was not in a hurry, but he maintains the friendship. This will give him an ample time to study the person very well and know if they are real or not. This time also will be valuable to him as they will be more eager to please and woo her. If he finally decides to open up for any of them, he doesn't publicize it by posting about it. He was on that platform for business and he needs as many "customers" as possible. Being private about it and indirectly suggests to them to keep what was going between them a secret. If not, other potential victims will take off. They need to live in the illusion that she is not taken yet. This will give him the opportunity to trap as many victims as possible in his cobweb of scam.

When he finally gets into serious commitment with them, he allows them to always start up the conversation. Letting them be on the driving seat but he must subtly control how they steer the ship in the friendship. This is typical of ladies. The scammer knows he must act that way. They are usually going to ask for other ways to reach her other than the usual chats. If the online platform allows audio or video calling, they are bound to call him. Since he is a man posing as a woman he wouldn't answer the call to prevent his victims from finding out his true identity.

He comes up with some really good excuse why he can't answer such calls. He could tell them her place of work doesn't allow workers answering phone or video calls. Some will want to find out when she is usually at home so as to call her during such free time, because no one works round the clock. In this case, he tells them but he will not come online those periods of time. This will give the impression that she is always exhausted after work and rests at home. In conclusion she doesn't have time. This is a perfect excuse for awhile.

But if things really get intense and serious, the victims will need her phone number. He is not in the place or country he claims to be, so getting their local phone number becomes the issue. But it's just simple for the experts. There are so many Apps that offer such services. Some of them are entirely free or relatively cheap. With that he can have the local phone number of any country in the world.

All he needs is a good and strong internet connection to use such numbers. Since he is a man and wouldn't want his masculine voice spoil things for him, he gets them to text him instead of calling. In the event they insist on hearing her voice he has no option than to buy a voice changer. With this tool he can twist his voice to sound feminine. When doing so, he doesn't prolong the call. He keeps it short to avoid getting caught. Such tools are usually not 100% efficient as their manufacturers want you to believe. The con man understands the importance of playing safe. If he cannot get such tools, getting a real girl to make the call is the second best option.

It will make the whole thing look real. All he needs to do is to intimate the girl with what she will say and not say. If possible draft an essay, putting down word to word all she needs to say. While making such calls, he puts it on loud speaker to help monitor the call. He can easily control things by signaling her when to keep quiet and when to talk. She must really sound sexy for the sexually perverted men. Then she also sounds official and responsible for the responsible ones. In all, her voice must blend into the occasion.

If it calls for video calling and it becomes mandatory for him to do so, they are Apps that people don't know exist that will assist him. Most people know and use such Apps without knowing its full potency in the criminal world. With such Apps he can load the person's pre-recorded video and allow it to play. Then play it for few seconds and ends it. When the victims ask what happened, he is usually very quick to blame the internet connectivity.

Most times once they have seen such short video they are usually convinced that she is real. If it's a nude video, it will get the man's head popping.

However, if the scammer chose to impersonate a man, then he needs to be ready to act like a man in need of love. First, he searches on different platforms on the internet for a suitable person to impersonate. He is very careful in putting some small details into consideration. These details if neglected will spell his doom in the con venture. So he doesn't leave anything to chance. He has to consider the age, race and physical appearance. At what age would a man be and he will be easily attractive to women on the internet.

What race is easier to find women tripping for them? And the physique is also very vital too. He cannot look dull and be sexually appealing to women. He has to find that handsome man with good physique. It's not compulsory he must be athletic. An average healthy looking man will fit into what the scammer is looking for. As a professional he doesn't go impersonating someone popular. He makes sure he changes their name, location and all the details about them. All he wants is their pictures and videos.

When he has seen a good example of this, he will proceed to creating a profile on any social media platform or in an online dating site. Dating sites are usually easier and better. Their double ganger is mostly likely not on such dating platforms. If he is truly handsome, ladies in real life will flock around him so much that he will hardly have extra time to look for love on the internet. This will act in the con man's favor by making sure his cover doesn't get blown.

Because if the person were to see that someone was using his pictures on a different name, they will not hesitate to report. And in most cases they don't stop until that fake profile is closed. A good con man doesn't want someone fighting to undermine their con. He is particularly careful to avoid them, as he goes for platforms that will not expose him. It will be painful to spend his time and energy trying to con his victim for months only for him to be exposed before getting paid. Prevention they say is better than cure and that rule is applicable in the con world too.

When they have carefully selected which platform to use, they need to make their profile look very real. As such they study the place and country they choose to pretend to be at. They also know the profession they claim to practice. They don't just come up with ambiguous details that they cannot live up to. They completely put their soul in it. Since they are looking for love, they always align their profile to reflect that. The con man could always indicate on his profile that he is single or divorced.

He is never in a rush in adding or accepting friends. He doesn't go about wasting his time on married women or teenagers. They are not what he needs in the scheme to be successful. The people he focuses his attention on are widows and single ladies. Mature ladies that are up to the age of tying the knot. He looks for widows or divorced single mothers. They are exactly in the category of being potential victims. The con man doesn't over add or request to be friends with this category of people at once to avoid being blocked by the social media platform as part of security measures employed by the site to prevent spamming.

He looks out for the fat and ugly ladies. The old ladies too who are lonely, retired and staying alone, category of people who will not have men making advances on them. Such people are secretly craving for attention and love. When the con man provides them with that, they will cross the red sea to please and do whatever he wants. So he is completely in for such people and the whole process is usually easy for him. He does everything to cut attention by posting good and enticing things. As ladies they are, they will not likely approach him first. So he understands he really has a lot of work to do by making them notice him.

He needs to often comment on their posts, always gracious and generous with his compliments. Finding a way to always align himself with his potential victims' opinion, but never too direct as to create the impression he was solely seeking their attention. With time, he tries and slide into their private message with "Hi "or "Hello". If they respond to him, he doesn't make the conversation about himself. He will do everything necessary to draw them out from their shell. Allowing them bare their hearts out as such people are most likely looking for someone to talk to. So the scammer tries to be that very person by being attentive to them.

The fraudster can't talk or discuss everything in one day. He must be patient to allow the concept of time to work its natural beauty. Occasionally, trying to find out how they were doing. They are women and prone to pride, he needs to be the one to start the chat. With time if they start liking him, then they will start participating actively. At this time he seeks for ways to communicate to them outside the platform he met them. Anyone who really likes him will want him to be in their life by giving him other ways of reaching out to them. It could be a phone number, email or anther social media platform.

Whichever one it is, he has to be the first to ask for it as an insurance policy. Just in case his fake profile gets blocked, which most times was likely going to happen. To the victim, the con man is just a caring man who wants other means to reach her always. The scammer must have created an email address to match their fake name. If she gives him an email address, she is probably going to be looking at such little details to see if his story checks out. A good con man will not ignore that because such things will make his mark suspicious of him. He would mail her regularly with romantic messages that she can't get elsewhere. If he is a good writer, he would compose such messages by himself. If not there are so many free sites that give him access to such messages.

If his victims give him their mobile phone number which is most likely, he needs to have gotten a local phone number in the country he claims to be in. Some free or paid Apps will give him this in less than ten minutes. He would text her more often with romantic words. Since the scammer is not from where he says he is from, chances are that his accent is different. The con man will try everything possible to avoid calls. If she insists and he has no option, then he tries to imitate the accent. In most cases, she will find out. The con man will quickly claim to have dual citizenship with a country that has entirely different accent and language. If she wants a video call, they are still Apps that will help him do that. He could also use two smart phones in faking a video call.

This actually requires high level of mastery. The procedure is complicated but can be learnt through practice. But he must always avoid audio calls and video calls. The con man concentrates more on chats and mailing. He keeps showering the victim with love and care by staying online always. He makes sure he is available to respond to them when they ever choose to.

This very scam is very complicated and unbelievable. It's difficult to convince people on the possibility of criminals compromising the bank security. Banks are like the most secured institutions in the world. For me to tell you that con men can actually break into any bank in the world sounds a little odd. But the truth is that they can actually do that by just simply creating a spam or phishing page of the bank.

The spam page basically means the exact replica of an original page hosted on a different domain name. For instance if the bank name is example.com their scam page can be esample.com. This will make it very difficult to spot the difference. The content of the page is exactly the same, no difference. So no one will suspect a thing. In order to make sure people log in to their scam page, these scammers will send them link. Since they have been in contact with them, the victim will trust the con man or woman by clicking on the link because it's all but similar to the original page.

If really the page is good and looks like the original one their victim will easily fall for their scheming. All they need to do is to create a perfect story to lure them. It could be the story on how they are unable to access their bank account because they were presently at some bank restricted area or region. The scammers will create the impression they needed the money in their account to do some quick transactions or invest in a business opportunity. They just come up with something very convincing and having chatted with the victims for a while, the con man most likely know how they react to issues.

Over the time in the course of their affair with the victims, they need to pick their brains by predicting them. It's not a difficult task because human beings follow a certain pattern which is known as habit. With this advantage, the con man could easily deduce beforehand if the victim will fall for it or not. If they will, what kind of story will make them fall is also vital.

When the victims finally agree, the scammer gives them his user name and password together with the link. Once they follow the link they will see his account balance running into millions. This will really make them go gaga in excitement. They will trust him the more for trusting them with his bank account details. Some will try to outsmart the con man at this stage by trying to move the whole money into their own account.

But the con man was prepared for this, by coding the page to inform them they cannot make any transaction. The page will alert them of the temporary suspension of the account due to the owner was trying to access it from overseas. There are other pop up messages the scammer could encode in it. All he wants at the end is to make them pay a certain percentage of the account balance in order to lift the suspension.

They will not hesitate to pay through any means the scammer's fake bank tells them to. Some will do so in a bid to take the whole money and disappear. This is human nature; they want to scam the scammer without knowing they are being scammed. Others will pay the money out of the love and trust they have for the con man. Trust me, which ever reason that they feel compelled to pay is nothing compared to the compelling powers of money. Money brings motivation and that fake big account balance is a bigger motivation. Who doesn't want to affiliate with the rich? Absolutely nobody! It will take a chronic cynical person to resist this costly temptation. If they are cynical, then the con man knows beforehand there is no need trying to con them in the first place. They don't waste their time on such people in their line of work.

CHAPTER TEN

MOBILE DEPOSIT

ACH

CREDIT CARD

All these categories fall within the type of scam that thrives on ease of transaction in banks. They are capitalizing on the trust that exists between bank and their customers. The fact that customers can actually request for loan or lodge in check without physically going to the bank. This very method has made it possible for dubious entities and scammers to rob people and bank of millions without actually being present in the country where the scam takes place.

All they need to do is gain your trust and possibly make you fall in love with them on social media. They impersonate someone that reflects the need and desire you want, they want you to easily fall in love with them by going through their profile. They will come up with the stories that they are currently in place where they cannot do video calls. But they will bombard you with chat and text messages. Since possibly you're seeking love, you are most likely going to fall under their spell.

To perfect this scam, they will tell you they need to transfer money or one kind of transaction that required you give them bank your username and password. They will also ask for your social security numbers, identity card, proof of address and other official documents. They also will tell you to be online for you to send them some OTP code that will make their transaction go through. With all these they can apply for bank loan without you knowing or they can do other forms of transactions that will affect you later.

In bill pay check, all they need is to get your address and phone number. Then they will buy a bank log of some company. From there, they will send like two thousand dollars check to you which will be delivered to your door stop after 3-5 days. They will ask you to proceed to the ATM to pay in the check into your bank account and subsequently send the money to them. You absolutely feel they sent you a legit check but after some time when the hacked company where the check came from finds out, you will pay back the money you sent to the scammers. Most times they can keep sending you two thousand dollars as many times as possible. Before your bank discovers the thing going on you already owe as much as ten thousand dollars. The con man can always give you like 10% of each transaction as a token for the work you are doing for them. You are completely unaware that it's all but your money.

Credit card fraud is a very popular form of online scam and does assume so many formats. These scammers are unfortunately really smart; they apply all sorts of means. They can hack your credit card through public hotspot, email and most times call you on the phone pretending to be your credit card issuer. You could easily fall for any of these means. This form of scam is so rampant that these criminals can actually have credit cards by just setting up a phishing page. When they succeed in getting all the information they want from you to compromise your credit card, some will sell it on numerous dark websites. There is no limit they can't go to get these details and they are many criminal elements ready to buy these details.

They can as well use phony calls. All they need to do is to get your phone number and call you to inform you that your credit card has been compromised by some hackers. During the call, they will claim to be from the credit card fraud department, they will ask you to provide them with some vital information regarding your credit card. You being anxious and wary for your card safety usually will not hesitate to spill the beans. They could also claim to have noticed some discrepancies in some charges which were made on your account that is tied to your credit card. To rectify this problem, they need you to provide your credit card details.

Naturally, as an innocent person you are going to succumb to this trick. They really sound very confident and official. To do this they will have all information and know the exact ethics that a call desk agent of a Credit Card Company will exhibit if they were to call their customer for a related case. They can even pretend to be calling you to inform you that the payment you made didn't go through if you were to visit an establishment where you used the card. To cross check what they have in the system they will tell you to provide your details. You being innocent minded who doesn't want to defraud the establishment will hastily give them the information they ask for.

But the most common means they employ is using emails. They will send you an email that looks more like an official email asking you to update your sensitive information to avoid your credit card from being blocked. They will usually threaten you with a deadline date. This is just to coerce you into hurrying because their scam page is usually hosted on a platform that does not last long. For you, they are protecting your interest so as to avoid your card from being suspended.

Sometimes, someone close to you with malicious intent can con you into revealing the sensitive information on your credit card. To those who enjoy free hotspots, using them could be counterproductive to you. If you log in to such public hotspots and subsequently access your credit card, they will steal it instantly. Because they have programmed it to fetch your credit card information and other related information. With these they can really harm you financially.

Some sites will claim to be running lottery and ask people to put their card details for an entry fee of as low as one dollar. Once you have given your information to them, they will make some transactions with your card without your consent. It's possible because at the point you were entering your details for the one dollar fee you got an OTP code. Once you authorize the code, you have relinquished your privacy to that site. They now possessed the authority to do anything without your financial institution alerting you to ask for your permission. It's assumed you have already given the permission. Credit Card fraudsters use this technique too. What they need is to get your information and transfer a small amount to you. Then place a phony call to you, pretending to be calling from your bank.

In that call, they will tell you that someone mistakenly paid into your account and they would like you to transfer the money back to the person. You being an innocent man with honorable intent will oblige. In doing such transfer, the bank will send you an OTP to your mobile number asking for your authorization. Once you authorize that transaction, the hacker will log into your bank account and add that person you transferred the money to your list. Once that's done, they will quickly move your money to that very account without the bank sending you a notification for authorization.

Some will create a charity organization, pretending to be helping the poor and needy. In doing so, they would make their donation channel to accept credit card that doesn't require verification by visa. With this, they can easily buy credit card information from dark webs. With those stolen cards they make donations on such fake charity sites. Some will even donate to a real charity site with a stolen credit card and ask the organization to return some part of the donated money.

They will claim they made mistake in typing a larger amount. Most real charity organizations are too honorable as they will oblige and send to the scammer back the money in a different account he chooses. This can also take place in hotels and in private jet booking. When they steal the credit card information, they make a booking to either a seven star hotel or to a private jet hiring company. When that's done, they will make a late cancellation of their booking which entails the money returned to them to a bank account they provide.

Fake check scams

Sometimes, someone out of the blue will offer to give you a certain amount of money. In the end they will send double of what they promised in check to you and subsequently ask you to wire back to them the excess. They could also beg you to assist them pay someone for a certain service. But instead of giving the exact amount, they will send you excess amount in check. They could also search through sites where consumers can easily resale their used products.

On such platforms they will make contact and indicate interest to buy your product which you have put up for sale. Just like in previous cases mentioned, they will send excess amount in check to you. Nevertheless, the bank clears and credits your account even when it is faked, once the check looks real enough to fool the banker. And these scammers are also perfect in their line of dirty work that it will take several weeks for the bank to detect the fraud. Once they do the innocent victim is made to pay back all or get sued.

Automated Clearing Housing

What the scammers do is to take advantage of the fact that ACH is a computer-based clearing and settlement facility established to process the exchange of electronic transactions between participating depository institutions. They use this to steal money from the bank accounts of innocent victims. It is easier for them since the ACH is based on network which is mostly used by financial institutions to take care of checks, cash transfers and direct deposit either occurring between individuals or institutions.

All they do is to lay their hands on your checking account number and routing number. They can get these details by dating you online, sending you phishing link or other means that will make you not to suspect their intentions. When they do they can easily pay bills and make payments by giving the receiver your routing number and checking account number.

CONCLUSION

What and people to avoid on the internet

As an internet user try to avoid fakers who in their fake lifestyle show glamour bereft of reality. They showcase their glamorously glittering shadow with no substance of gold. Don't get depressed when you see people post pictures of them having exquisite meals in some fancy locations. Such meals most likely have the exact nutritional content with your one dollar meal, if not less.

Don't feel down when they show off designers clothes bought on credit as though your non-designer clothes are not covering your nakedness. The essence of clothing is to cover one's body from the shame of walking about naked. You can still look super cool with your "cheap" clothes. Dressing smart does not entail dressing up in million dollar worth of clothes. They take pictures at airport near private jets even when they are not flying in it, all in a bid to portray a lavish lifestyle. Imagine if super rich billionaires took pictures of themselves each time they boarded their state of the art aircraft.

What am saying in essence is that, true rich people are not in the business of posting pictures to impress. The media and paparazzi jostle to take such shots. Fakers hold stack of dollar bills to their ear on Instagram. Imagine if Bill Gates decided to hold all his money to his ear just to take a selfie. Don't fall for the antics of those who have no life outside the fake life they live on the social media. Don't kill yourself, they are probably more broke than you are. Don't be deceived, no one's life is better than yours. Your life is exactly where and how you consciously or unconsciously kept it. Only you can make it better not to surpass anyone's but to surpass what it was.

This is another form of online scam, the type of scam that rubs you off your emotional confidence. This kind of scam is worst because it actually goes unpunished. No legal implications to their heinous crimes. Some of them are aware of what they do and others are not. As negligible their actions might be, it is rather very disastrous. They are doing so much harm on the internet.

Silently they kill people daily with their attitude, what they post and how they react to other people's posts. In order to promote their fake life style they ruin others. It's just always about them. Too selfish to the core and you begin to wonder if they had any human heart in them. The worst of it all is that their victims are perpetually tied to their rope of scam and deceit. Some will never know the impact of what these criminals do to them until it's too late. Others don't even acknowledge that these people are their enemies.

These enemies are people who are on various online platforms doing things that will arouse envy from others. Constantly, they post pictures of where they are having a good time. These pictures are so many and keep coming endlessly. Thus, making it look like it's the truth on how they actually live. Everything about them they paint it with smiles. Even when they cry, they are posting things to suggest otherwise.

They use their last penny to buy clothes just to make them look super good. Some will go to the extent of borrowing to achieve that. All this is just to impress and to oppress others. Making others look unhappy in their private lives. These emotional criminals pretend to have the best relationship and marriage, even when they are going through nightmare in such affairs. To keep up the lie, they keep posting pictures of their little happy time together with their spouse. Posting and lying how financially stable they are even when they are broke. Fakers and liars is what they are!

With time you could start feeling jealous and really wants your life to be like theirs, unknowingly striving to be them. You could start posting things that will make you look super rich even when you got nothing. You have been scammed emotionally. To the internet bullies, those who are constantly bullying others with their words, making them feel disadvantaged because of one reason or another. Such people deserve a place in the prison yard. They are essentially the cause of rampant suicide in the world today. Try also to avoid getting into political arguments as much as possible.

You might think it's wise when you engage in too much activism. But it's not so because it starts to take its toll on you. Most of these political arguments end with you saying negative things about some politicians or persons whose opinion contradicts yours. Imagine you spending most of your day yelling and cursing people online. The impact it does to your inner spirit is very enormous. You're so soaked in negativity that you start attracting negative things to your life. You really become a bitter person to that effect.

Politicians will always have a way to settle their differences. They do that secretly, over the dinner table, fundraising events and others. They are always about their selfish interests. To them is all about self preservation.

But you as their ardent follower are perpetually at logger heads with your neighbor because he supports a different politician. You're killing yourself! Have you noticed that these people you fight for rarely have their children fight for them? Why then do you want to kill yourself for someone whose kids are enjoying the wealth your struggle brings to their parents? As voters, we can still indulge in politics without having to hate one another. Hate is like a stain on a white piece of cloth. Just a drop of it renders that piece imperfect. It's wrong to give in to hate. You can argue less on social media platforms and proffer solutions in polite ways. It is for your own good to be happy always, don't let politics rob you off that chance. Politics is so laced up with complications that no one is truly right. People will keep having their divergent opinion.

Reveal less about your personal life on your profile. You might get attacked by that. Posting up to date pictures about you is fun until your life becomes a public toilet. Everyone can tell how you look like and what you could do at every minute. You have made your life an open investigation.

www.ingramcontent.com/pod-product-compliance
Lightning Source LLC
Chambersburg PA
CBHW031239050326
40690CB00007B/875